Citizenship in Schools

edited by
Ken Fogelman

D0453319

David Fulton Publishers
London

David Fulton Publishers Ltd
2 Barbon Close, London WC1N 3JX

First published in Great Britain by
David Fulton Publishers 1991

Note: The right of the authors to be identified as the authors of this work has
been asserted by them in accordance with the Copyright, Designs and Patents Act
1988.

British Library Cataloguing in Publication Data

Citizenship in schools.
  I. Fogelman, Ken, *1945–*
  370.1150941

ISBN 1-85346-160-1

Typeset by Chapterhouse, Formby L37 3PX
Printed in Great Britain by
BPCC Wheaton Ltd. Exeter.

Contents

Contributors .... See inside back cover

Foreword iv

1 Introduction – Citizenship in Schools 1
Ken Fogelman

2 The Work of the Speaker's Commission and its Definition
of Citizenship 6
Frances Morrell

3 Active Citizenship and Young People 17
Janet Edwards and Ken Fogelman

4 Citizenship in Secondary Schools: The National Picture 35
Ken Fogelman

5 Approaches to Citizenship 49
Meriel Vlaeminke and Max Burkimsher

6 The Dukeries Community College and Complex: A Case
Study 64
Roy Sowden and Lewis Walker

7 Citizenship in Schools 76
George Gyte and Danielle Hill

8 Citizenship Education 92
Val Lynch and Keith Smalley

9 Citizenship in Schools: A Political Perspective 113
Andrew Rowe MP

Mr Speaker

Speaker's House Westminster London SW1A 0AA

Foreword

by The Right Honourable Bernard Weatherill, M.P.
Speaker of the House of Commons

In my foreword to **Encouraging Citizenship,** the report of the Commission on
Citizenship, I placed special emphasis on the needs of young people and the
role of schools.   I also acknowledged the pioneering work undertaken by the
Commission's education team based at Leicester University.   As I wrote,
citizenship, like anything else, has to be learned; young people do not
become good citizens by accident.

Such exhortations can only be the first step.   At a time when teachers are
being asked to respond to so many new initiatives, it is not enough simply to
add yet another expectation upon them.   It is important also to demonstrate
how the ways in which schools approach citizenship will be of benefit to, and
can be integrated with, their other activities, in addition to contributing
to the development of our young citizens and our future society.

For these reasons I particularly welcome this book.   In part it is based on
the work which was carried out for the Commission at Leicester University, but
with more detailed accounts of that research than it was possible to include in
the Commission's report.   However, other chapters describe philosophies,
activities and approaches which are being developed in particular schools and
local authorities.   These contributions make it possible to see how the ideas
put forward by the Commission can be put into practice constructively and
imaginatively, often by building upon what is already taking place within our
schools.   The links with other cross-curricular themes and other elements
of the national Curriculum become clearer, and citizenship can be seen as a
liberalising and liberating part of the cirriculum, rather than just another
topic to be delivered.

The test of our ideas on citizenship, and of the educational response to them,
will come in the future, when new generations of young citizens have passed through
our schools.   In the meantime, it is for teachers and others working with
young people to provide the ideas and experiences which will lead to success in
this venture.   I hope that they will find in this book part of the support
which they deserve, to help them in this important task.

Bernard Weatherill

CHAPTER 1

Introduction – Citizenship in Schools

Ken Fogelman

It is in the last two years that the term 'citizenship' has started to become familiar and to feel important for our schools. Of course neither the word nor many of the activities which it is now seen to encompass are new in education. The chapter in this book by Edwards and Fogelman identifies books which have been written on the subject since the early years of this century. Similarly, many schools have been fostering community and other relevant activities for many years.

However, until recently citizenship in schools was largely synonymous with civics and teaching about the British constitution. Whilst these aspects are not irrelevant, the concept has now broadened, not only to include a much wider body of knowledge, but also issues of attitudes, personal skills and participation. The origins of this change, and the movement of citizenship to somewhere near the centre of the educational stage, can be located in a number of places, but two are particularly important. First, there has been concern about the political and community knowledge, commitment and involvement of young people in our society – and not only young people. This strand is well articulated by Andrew Rowe in his chapter in this book. Again, this is hardly a new concern, but on this occasion it was picked up constructively and enthusiastically at the political level, leading to the establishment of the Commission on Citizenship under the patronage of Bernard Weatherill, Speaker of the House of Commons.

The second major element is the introduction of the National Curriculum in all our maintained schools. Although the National Curriculum itself is conceived in terms of the ten core and foundation subjects, it is only a part, albeit the major part, of what is now known as 'the whole curriculum'. National Curriculum Council Circular No. 6 (October, 1989) and Curriculum Guidance No. 3 (March, 1990) discussed and set out the cross-curricular elements which are to be seen as an essential part of the whole curriculum. They included the five cross-curricular themes: economic and industrial understanding; careers education and guidance; health education; environmental education; and education for citizenship.

Thus, it is no longer acceptable for citizenship in schools to be dependent on the enthusiasm of particular teachers for teaching about politics or the law, or for providing some of their pupils with the experience of community service. Rather, it is part of the entitlement of all young people in our schools, from 5 to 16 at least. Schools are faced with the challenge of deciding, with guidance from the NCC and others, what they should be doing under the heading of citizenship; identifying what they are already doing and where the gaps are; planning the experiences and activities which will meet these gaps; and ensuring continuity and progression in their students' experiences throughout their years in school.

Fortunately, of the many changes and innovations faced by schools in recent times, there are few where so much preparatory thinking has been done. Most notably, there is the work and report of the Speaker's Commission, which are described by Frances Morrell in the next chapter. As indicated there, the Commission's initial focus was on 'active citizenship' and voluntary participation, but its scope broadened and education became a particular focus.

In the period when citizenship as a cross-curricular theme was first being discussed, there was some nervousness that schools might be asked to take up too narrow a conception. Those of us involved with the Commission's working party on citizenship and schools were concerned that this should not be the case; that its fullest interpretation and application should be recognized. In the words of the Commission's evidence which it submitted to the National Curriculum Council, the study of citizenship should not be ' . . . vulnerable either to being presented as theory without practice, as in civics courses, or to being offered solely as an experience, as practice without theory'.

The Commission's evidence therefore emphasized four elements as being necessary. These included the acquisition of a body of knowledge, but equally important are: understanding the rules; the development and exercise of skills; and learning democratic behaviour through experience of the school as a community, and from the experience of the school as an institution playing a role in the wider community.

Happily, when NCC Curriculum Guidance No. 8 appeared in November, 1990 (after several of the chapters in this book had been prepared) it reflected a similarly broad view of education for citizenship. Rightly included, indeed first, in its framework and objectives is knowledge (and understanding): of the nature of community; of roles and relationships in a democratic society; and of the nature and basis of duties, responsibilities and rights. But also emphasized as underpinning education for citizenship are skills: communication, numeracy, study, problem-solving, personal and social, and information technology. Furthermore, and very importantly, there is recognition of the links with and implications for the wider school context. In the section on policy and planning there is reference to the relevance to other aspects of school policy and life: behaviour, equal opportunities, community relations, recording and reporting achievement, pupil welfare, staff welfare, extra-curricular activities, teaching methods, classroom organization, organization and management of the school, and school ethos. This formidable list would suggest that there is very little happening in schools to which citizenship education is not related.

This book appears, therefore, at a point where the framework, aims and objectives of education for citizenship are reasonably clear. It is not a textbook of materials for the teaching of citizenship, although it does contain many practical ideas and suggestions based on what is already happening in some schools. These are particularly to be found in the chapter by Vlaeminke and Burkimsher, in the case studies at the end of the chapter by Lynch and Smalley, and in Sowden and Walker's account of the Dukeries Community College. However, the prime purpose of this book is to assist those in schools, authorities and in teacher training who are now having to think about the implementation of citizenship education, perhaps for the first time. Many will prefer to tailor the detail of their response to the strengths and local circumstances of their own institution or group of institutions, but all will need to clarify their philosophies and policies from which the detail derives; and all will need to tackle such issues as management and organization, monitoring, assessment and reporting, continuity and progression. And, of course, these issues are equally as relevant to the other cross-curricular themes as they are to citizenship.

The first three chapters after this introduction set the scene, and are in a sense historical. First, as mentioned, Frances Morrell provides us with an account of the work of the Commission on Citizenship and its report, setting the educational issues in the broader context within which the Commission was working. In particular, she describes the definition of citizenship formulated by the Commission and discusses some of its implications.

The chapter by Janet Edwards and myself is based on part of a review of evidence on active citizenship undertaken for the Commission. It describes earlier major documents relevant to citizenship and young people, as well as some of the pioneering efforts of schools which pre-dated, and no doubt influenced, the recent rise in interest. In addition, we indicate some of the other organizations concerned with, or offering activities or resources relevant to, the experiences of young people within and beyond school, particularly in the areas of community and voluntary service.

In the fourth chapter I summarize the findings of a national survey of citizenship in secondary schools, carried out in collaboration with Social and Community Planning Research, for the Speaker's Commission. The survey's findings are important in demonstrating that many schools are already enthusiastic about citizenship and have vigorous programmes in place, but that, taken overall, the national picture is piecemeal and patchy. In addition, some of the findings, which are reported for the first time in Chapter 4, begin to point to some of the particular issues which schools will have to consider and monitor, where their circumstances or traditions may initially hinder some aspects of their approach to citizenship.

The next two chapters give a more direct and deeper account of the approaches of particular schools. Mel Vlaeminke and Max Burkimsher carried out a further piece of work undertaken for the Speaker's Commission, entailing a more qualitative study of selected schools in Leicestershire and Northamptonshire. They talked with heads, other staff and students, and observed lessons and other activities as they took place. The interactions among ethos, planning and imaginative activities are made very clear. I felt it important that there should be space in this book for one deeper and fuller account of the approach of a single institution, and this is provided by Roy Sowden and Lewis Walker. The Dukeries Complex in Nottinghamshire is a Community College, but also a great deal more. The chapter describes the context, the underlying philosophy of community, historical development and management issues, as well as a range of fascinating activities.

Northamptonshire and Leicestershire are certainly two of those counties which were thinking about and fostering citizenship education before it was ever mentioned by the National Curriculum Council. George Gyte and Danielle Hill from Northamptonshire, in addition to a discussion specific to citizenship, consider the inter-relationships of all five cross-curricular themes and the role of personal and social education. They offer a model which integrates these, with citizenship at the core.

Val Lynch and Keith Smalley provide a detailed analysis of each element in citizenship education and the relationship of those elements to core and foundation subjects and to issues in assessment. They discuss one important element which has not been mentioned previously in this introduction – respect for other people. Their chapter concludes with brief case studies of eight Leicestershire schools.

Despite all this evidence of the potential benefits of citizenship education, some readers may remain uncertain of the political implications of citizenship education. Why has the concept been taken up with such apparent enthusiasm by so many politicians? Does it derive from a particular political perspective? Or do politicians see an opportunity to instil attitudes in our young people which increase the likelihood of them voting in a particular way? While these are dangers about which we should remain vigilant, the chapter by Andrew Rowe MP demonstrates that the case can be well made in a non-partisan way.

Above all, I hope that this book conveys some of the excitement associated with the development of citizenship education. Precisely because it impinges on so many aspects of school life and beyond, its potential effects and benefits are far-reaching. There is much still to be done, but much to be gained from doing it well. That is why we have now established the Centre for Citizenship Studies in Education at the University of Leicester School of Education, and we look forward to working with colleagues throughout the education service to assist schools in their implementation of citizenship, the other cross-curricular elements and the whole curriculum.

CHAPTER 2

The Work of the Speaker's Commission and its Definition of Citizenship

Frances Morrell

Irrelevant subjects like horse-riding and citizenship were to be expunged from the curriculum. This, according to one newspaper, was the intention of the Department of Education and Science at the time that the Commission on Citizenship was being established under the patronage of the Rt Hon. Bernard Weatherill MP, Speaker of the House of Commons.

Today, the National Curriculum Council's guidance on Education for Citizenship has been sent to every school. The Prime Minister, John Major MP has promised a 'citizen's charter'. Powerful forces within the European Community are advocating the creation of a 'Citizen's Europe' to match the single market.

In retrospect, the Commission on Citizenship was a little ahead of its time and was able, through its work, to contribute to the recognition of citizenship as a theme within the United Kingdom and quietly to influence the development of public policy, particularly so far as education is concerned.

What was the purpose of the Commission when it was established? What does citizenship mean and why does it matter? The Commission was established in the first instance to examine ways in which individuals could be enabled to participate fully and effectively in the community. This objective of encouraging citizenship reflected the concern of the Commission's patron, Bernard Weatherill MP, that many young people he met seemed to have little idea of how they were governed or what part they might play in the process:

> I believe that citizenship, like anything else has to be learned. Young people do not become good citizens by accident any more than they become good nurses or good engineers or good bus drivers or computer scientists. My concern [is] whether we offer enough encouragement to our young people to learn how to be good citizens (Commission on Citizenship, 1990).

A second area of interest to the Commission was that of voluntary participation in the community by agencies, voluntary bodies and volunteers and the relationship of this kind of participation to the more traditional notions of citizenship involving, for example, the exercise of the right to vote or the right to a fair trial. Bodies like Community Service Volunteers were concerned that this kind of contribution should be more widely recognized and encouraged.

Perhaps underlying these concerns there was a deeper worry not expressed at the outset but which became clearer to Commission members as their work progressed. This was a sense that our society is not simply a by-product of our activities as consumers or family members. Wealth creation, the relationship between management, workers and consumers is one vital subject of modern political debate. The rules, responsibilities and roles within the family are another. But the role of individuals as citizens within the public or political community is different again: it was this third dimension which Commission members felt was both as important as wealth creation and family life and in danger of neglect:

> A variety of active organisations are the key to ... democracy. Through active involvement in common concerns, the citizen can overcome the sense of relative isolation and powerlessness that results from the insecurity of life in an increasingly commercial society. Associations along with decentralised local administration mediate between the individual and the centralised state, providing forums in which opinion can be publicly and intelligently shaped and the subtle habits of public initiative and responsibility learned and passed on. Associational life, in Tocqueville's thinking, is the best bulwark against the condition he feared most: the mass society of mutually antagonistic individuals, easy prey to despotism. These intermediate structures check and restrain the tendencies of centralised government to assume more and more administrative control (Bellah *et al.*, 1985: 38).

But what did the Commission mean by citizenship: the difficulty of defining the term preoccupied members for the first months of their work together.

At a seminar, members considered papers presented by Sir Ralf Dahrendorf, Professor Norman Barrie, Professor Raymond Plant, Roger Henderson QC and Paul Boateng MP. Two separate pieces of research were commissioned. The first, on the views of young people, by Ann Richardson of Social and Community Planning Research (SCPR), was commissioned by the Prince's Trust and the Commission (Talking about Commitment, 1990). The second, a national survey of schools, was conducted by Professor Fogelman of Leicester University and Social and Community Planning Research. A paper setting out the Commission's approach was circulated widely on a consultative basis. At a later stage the Commission drew on a wide range of academic work, published and unpublished.

An immediate difficulty was that in our society the term 'citizenship' is an unfamiliar notion. Asked about it, young people 'almost invariably found themselves with a moment or more of embarrassed silence . . . the fact that the word "citizenship" is not in common use was frequently commented upon' (Richardson, 1990: 8).

As *Encouraging Citizenship* (Commission on Citizenship, 1990) describes, political philosophers suggested to the Commission that agreement on the meaning of citizenship in principle is very difficult:

> Trying to pin down the definition as the only true or real one is in itself a political activity because it brings into play a more general normative or ideological commitment within which an idea of citizenship sits as a part (Plant, 1989: 1).

Other thinkers argued that democracy itself is a sham. Citizens' actions, struggles and movements are assumed

> to reveal their impotence, dependency and in any case their ignorance in respect of the powers of such phenomena as the state's bureaucracy, the ruling groups and elites, dominant and mystifying ideologies and ultimately socio-economic forces (Roche, 1987: 363).

The research into the teaching of citizenship in schools established that, although many schools claimed to address the subject, there was 'an extraordinary multiplicity of interpretations of its meaning' (Fogelman, 1990: 5). Commission members were interested in the divisions among political philosophers and the relative lack of interest until recently on the part of academic theorists, in contrast to the deep concern of citizens themselves, in the nature of citizenship, citizen policies and citizen communities. Young people felt indignant at the failure to teach them about their citizenship and what it meant for them.

> It is unusual to find wide consensus on any issue. Yet in this study, there was one issue which united virtually everyone across the social spectrum. From those who had left school with few qualifications to those in university or beyond, there was a strong call for more teaching of the issues surrounding citizenship in schools.... One 17 year old put the argument this way: 'You should know about it – it's your life, it's your community – and you really have a responsibility to yourself to know about it' (Richardson, 1990: 35).

Commission members set out in the Report the background to their thinking. They were aware of the long tradition of Western thought about citizenship, from Aristotle's *Politics* – 'A citizen is one who has a share in both ruling and being ruled. Deliberative or judicial, we deem him to be a citizen' – to the writings of Cicero, Machiavelli, Burke, de Tocqueville, Mill and, in our own country, Hannah Arendt.

They considered that, for this country, any definition we adopted had to include legal membership of a political community based on universal suffrage and also membership of a civil community based on the rule of law. The definition, framework and approach to be found in the work of T. H. Marshall, whose classic theory was first published in 1950, seemed to us to provide a sensible starting point. Marshall's definition itself is an open one: it recognizes citizenship as a process. Marshall includes in his definition a social element and in doing so seems to reflect the British approach to citizenship. According to Marshall citizenship is:

> a status bestowed on those who are full members of a community. All who possess the status are equal with respect to the rights and duties with which that status is endowed. There is no universal principle that determines what those rights and duties shall be, but societies in which citizenship is a developing institution create an image of an ideal citizenship against which achievement can be directed.... The urge forward along the path thus plotted is an urge towards a fuller measure of equality, an enrichment of the stuff of which the status is made and an increase in the number of those on whom the status is bestowed.... Citizenship requires a ... direct sense of community membership based on loyalty to a civilisation which is a common possession. It is a loyalty of free men endowed with rights and protected by a common law. Its growth is stimulated both by the struggle to win those rights and by their enjoyment when won (Marshall, 1950: 28–9 and 40–1).

Marshall envisaged citizenship as involving three elements, civil, political and social which he argued were developed in successive centuries: civil rights in the eighteenth, political in the nineteenth and social in the twentieth.

> The civil element is composed of the rights necessary for individual freedom – liberty of the person, freedom of speech, thought and faith, the right to own property and to conclude valid contracts and the right to justice. The last is of a different order from the others because it is the right to defend and assert all one's rights on terms of equality with others and by due process of law. This shows us that the institutions most directly associated with civil rights are the courts of justice.
>
> By the political element I mean the right to participate in the exercise of political power, as a member of a body invested with political authority or as an elector of the members of such a body. The corresponding institutions are Parliament and councils of local government.
>
> By the social element I mean the whole range from the right to a modicum of economic welfare and security to the right to share to the full in the social heritage and to live the life of a civilised being according to the standards prevailing in the society. The institutions most closely connected with it are the education system and the social services (Marshall, 1950: 10–11).

How people define a citizenship

In working with partners on new initiatives, the Commission checked whether or not Marshall's approach represents their understanding of citizenship. The Commission's own consultative conference on citizenship in schools supported Marshall's definition, subject to updating the language. The quantitative research carried out by Richardson (1990) and Crewe (Johnston Conover et al., 1990) was also consistent with Marshall's approach to the social dimension of citizenship.

For young adults, being a citizen meant belonging, either as a result of nationality or through conforming to the laws and coming to be accepted – that is, by virtue of domicile. It involved rights such as 'the right to express your views without being in jail or shot'. Limits were set on the power of those in authority: 'They can't just chuck you in prison and forget about you . . . . They can only hold you for so long'. It also involved duties 'to pay taxes and abide by the law' (Richardson, 1990: 8).

Adults took a similarly phrased view of rights: 'the right not to be murdered'; 'the right not to be molested'; 'the right to expect others to be law-abiding' (Johnson Conover et al., 1990: 13). When asked directly what were the most important rights 'the majority of British citizens had no hesitation in according primacy to social rights . . . to a minimum standard of living, to medical care, to a job and to education' (p. 13). Those consulted agreed that 'rights are not universal, but instead depend on the country and the historical period in which one lives'. They are won by struggle, 'we are going back to the rights of every century when people have fought and died to give us our rights in this century' (p. 18). On responsibilities, the views of the British citizen were clear: 'Far and away the most commonly cited British duty, however, was obedience to the law . . . combined with a more general emphasis on civility or obedience to community norms' (p. 21).

The Commission's Report sets out a traditional British analysis of citizenship which seemed to match British people's perceptions of it. Certain terms in regular use in the discussion of citizenship are also regularly disputed. The Report makes clear what the Commission meant by rights, duties and obligations.

Rights

- *Rights are a set of entitlements.* They are a very precise concept, 'not one of moral exhortation but one of the realities of people's lives' (Dahrendorf, Commission on Citizenship: 2).
- *Rights are necessarily individual.* 'Although a limited company or a charitable foundation, such as your sponsors, can epitomise and espouse the characteristics of citizenship, neither can enjoy citizenship' (Henderson, unpublished paper: 2).
- *Rights are residual entitlements.* There is no accessible, comprehensive statement of the rights of citizens in the UK, such as is found in the constitutions of other countries. The foundation of government in the UK is the notion that Parliament is the supreme authority and that the validity of its legislation cannot therefore be challenged in the UK courts. As a result, the individual's freedoms are residual: that is, they exist to the extent that Parliament has not enacted restrictions and they are vulnerable to any subsequent enactment of Parliament.
- *Rights include social rights.* Supporters of the classical liberal perspective reject the concept of social rights because it undermines the market and the open society within which it is possible for individuals with differing ends and purposes to live together.

The Commission supported the analysis put forward by Dahrendorf: 'From an early point onwards in our century, more and more people came to believe that civil and political rights are not worth an awful lot unless they are backed up by a certain basic social security which enables people to make use of these rights and makes it impossible for others to push them around in such a way that the rights become an empty constitutional promise without any substance...a floor on which everyone stands and below which no one must fall' (Dahrendorf, Commission on Citizenship: 4).

In the UK there is no comprehensive constitutional list of entitlements. Individuals' freedoms exist to the extent that Parliament has not enacted restrictions. By the same token, there is no list of duties. However, citizens have a duty to respect the law. The duty to pay taxes, to serve on juries or to refrain from treasonable activities are examples of what is required of a citizen on this basis.

The Commission did not accept that there was a simple quid pro quo relationship – a bargain – between entitlements and duties for each individual citizen. This key issue was highlighted by a number of speakers. It agreed with Dahrendorf: 'There are rights of citizenship and there are [duties]. Both are absolutely valid if they are valid at all, but we shouldn't turn them into a quid pro quo' (Dahrendorf, Commission on Citizenship: 6). In other words, both exist in their own right; the relationship between them is far from simple.

The Commission distinguished between the entitlements and duties of citizenship and the obligations of institutions funded by the taxpayer which exist, in part, to give effect to the entitlements. Three sets of institutions – the courts, Parliament and local councils and the institutions of the education and social services – correspond respectively to the three kinds of entitlements: civil, political and social. Clearly, entitlements would not exist without institutions charged with the responsibility of giving them effect.

In analysing citizenship, therefore, the Commission considered in the first place the relationship between the entitlements and duties of the individual on the one hand and the corresponding obligations of public institutions on the other as well as the framework of rules to which they both conform. In a key qualification the Commission stressed:

> We do not believe that the whole exercise by citizens of their civil, political and social entitlements is contained within that formal structure, as the traditional analysis seems to suggest.

Encouraging Citizenship (Commission of Citizenship, 1990) argues that the voluntary contribution by individual citizens to the common good through participation in and exercise of civic duty and the encouragement of such activities by public and private institutions is a part of citizenship. Decentralized local administration and a variety of active organizations and opportunities for individual involvement are the key to democracy. Free associations, free trade unions and democratically elected local government represent collective rights held in common. Within the public or political community individuals consult and argue, listen and persuade and, in so doing, accept the idea of a public good that transcends the private.

The Report quotes Carole Pateman, a leading writer on this theme, who envisages a political community as a political association of a multiplicity of political associations. The members of the community are

> citizens in many . . . associations which are bound together through horizontal and multi-faceted tiers of self assumed political obligation. The essential feature . . . is that the political sphere is one dimension, the collective dimension of social life as a whole. It is the area of social existence in which citizens voluntarily co-operate together and sustain their common life and common undertaking (Pateman, 1979: 174).

Being a citizen involves, according to Marshall, 'belonging to a community', but he suggests that there are no 'universal principles' that determine what that entails. The legally defined national community is the most easily recognized society within which citizenship rights and duties exist. A British citizen is a member of a legally defined national community and should, in consequence of a long period of evolution, enjoy civil, political and social entitlements and duties that go with the status. Secondly, such entitlements and duties extend beyond national frontiers as the result of national membership of broader groups, for example, the European Community. Finally, we can speak of membership of a world community with rights in international law established in the post-war period.

The Commission agreed that there are no 'universal principles' analogous to the laws of science that determine what the status of membership of a community entails. In this context, two points were considered. In the Commission's view, one of the most important aspects of citizenship is that it involves the maintenance of an agreed framework of rules governing the relationships of individuals to the state and to one another. Secondly, each of those communities has developed a set of rules valid in law.

During the post-war period, the UK has agreed a number of declarations and conventions. These set out our principles on human rights, so far as the world community is concerned and also in relation to the European Community. All domestic political parties, for many decades, have accepted the UK's position with regard to these conventions. Indeed, the UK played a leading role in developing them: for example, as a drafting member of the Council of Europe which elaborated the European Convention on Human Rights and the first state to ratify the Convention.

The Universal Declaration of Human Rights was adopted by the United Nations in December 1948. The Declaration was the inspiration behind later multilateral human rights conventions and the inclusion in constitutions of newly emerged states of human rights guarantees. The European Convention on Human Rights came into force on 3 September 1953. These texts marked an alteration in the status of the individual in international law, recognizing the entitlements of individuals – their human rights – irrespective of their citizenship of a particular state; this co-called 'new citizenship' is discussed by Gardner (1990).

The European Social Charter, which is the counterpart of the European Convention on Human Rights in the sphere of economic and social rights, was signed at Turin on 18 October 1961 and came into force on 26 February 1965. The supervisory system under the Charter differs in important respects from that of the European Convention. The Charter makes no provision for binding decisions by judicial or quasi-judicial means. Individuals have no right of direct petition. However, both the Charter and the Convention recognize rights vested in the individual and not tied to the existence of any national affiliation.

The underlying principles of our own system of entitlements, duties and obligations of citizenship institutions are similar to those outlined in the conventions. For example, the rights to education and health treatment are based on residence rather than on nationality. European Community nationals have rights of movement and entitlements to social benefits which are, to an extent, attached to the individual. Accrued benefits can thus be retained when the individual moves from one member state to another.

Plainly the relationship between laws, rules, traditions and conventions is complicated. Terms such as 'human rights' and 'citizenship entitlements' overlap but do not have the same meaning. A technical review was outside the scope of this report. The simple point is that many individuals in the UK play an active role, through travel, work, leisure or community activity in more than one legally defined community.

The importance of rules

Finally the Commission considered that citizenship involves the perception and maintenance of an agreed framework of rules or guiding principles rather than shared values.

Such a framework of rules is more than a set of external texts whose legitimacy is acknowledged: an agreed framework of rules provides the shared basis whereby individuals relate day-to-day to the 'fellow strangers' of their community:

> there are more citizens in a nation state than any individual could meet, let alone get to know well in a life-time. They are not complete strangers however – as in the case of people from entirely different places and cultures... they are a community of fellow strangers (Roche, 1987: 376).

Belonging to a community involves at a minimum an understanding of the framework of rules or guiding principles that govern that community.

Why then does citizenship matter today? The context of the Commission's work was the great changes that have affected our society and the sense that change is taking place at a faster pace than ever before. The status and entitlements of individuals are directly affected by the UK's membership of the European Community and changed relationship with the Commonwealth. Again, since the war, Britain has been transformed into a multi-racial society. At the same time, shifts in the income, lifestyle, nature of work and demographic balance of the population are affecting people's expectations, traditional arrangements for working life, retirement and care in the community. All these matters impact directly on our citizenship arrangements. The Commission concluded that action was needed if citizens were to continue to enjoy their full legal and social rights. A review of the law relating to the legal rights and duties and entitlements of citizens in the UK was needed. A second review of the relationship between statutory and voluntary bodies was proposed. A key set of recommendations dealt with the need for citizenship to be a part of the education of every pupil from the early years right through to further and higher education.

The Commission recommended the establishment of an independent body 'charged with the specific responsibility to document and research social, economic and educational aspects of citizenship; to consider new legislation... to stimulate public discussion and to deal with all aspects of citizenship'.

16

References

Bellah, R. N., Madsen, R., Sullivan, W., Swidler, A. and Tipton, S. M. (1985) *Habits of the Heart*. London: University of California Press.

Commission on Citizenship (1990) *Encouraging Citizenship*. London: HMSO.

Dahrendorf, R. (1989) Paper presented to the Commission on Citizenship seminar, April.

Fogelman, K. (1990) 'Citizenship in secondary schools: a national survey', Appendix E, in Commission on Citizenship, *Encouraging Citizenship*. London: HMSO.

Gardner, P. (1990) 'What lawyers mean by citizenship', Appendix D in Commission on Citizenship, *Encouraging Citizenship*. London: HMSO.

Johnston Conover, P., Crewe, I. and Searing, D. (1990) 'The nature of citizenship in the United States and Great Britain: empirical comments on theoretical themes', *Journal of Politics*, **42**, 4.

Marshall, T. H. (1950) *Citizenship and Social Class*. Cambridge: Cambridge University Press.

Pateman, C. (1979) *The Problem of Political Obligation: A Critical Analysis of Liberal Theory*. London: John Wiley & Sons.

Plant, R. (1989) Paper presented to the Commission on Citizenship Seminar, April.

Richardson, A. (1990) *Talking about Commitment*. London: The Prince's Trust.

Roche, M. (1987) 'Citizenship, social theory and change', *Theory and Society*, **16**:363–99.

CHAPTER 3

Active Citizenship and Young People

Janet Edwards and Ken Fogelman

This chapter summarizes part of the review of research evidence on active citizenship undertaken for the Speaker's Commission. Specifically, it addresses those aspects which are concerned with young people.

We do not begin to claim that our work covered all the ways in which individuals and groups are involved in activities pertinent to people's roles as citizens. We offer here a summary of the way we see citizenship emerging in the curriculum of schools; some comments on the democratic involvement of young people in the organization of school life; and information on some organizations which seem to us to be involved in relevant activities with young people either within, over-lapping with, or outside schools and colleges.

Citizenship in the curriculum

The teaching of civics and citizenship in English schools is not a new phenomenon. Batho (1990) traces its progress from the Victorian period, noting particularly the 1930s as a decade when the teaching of citizenship was 'widely advocated and in many areas practised in secondary schools'. The 1940s saw a 'much increased awareness of world citizenship' but the 50s and 60s saw no universal acceptance of the importance of democratic education for all pupils and 'social studies, civics and citizenship became the province of the less able'. However, current affairs lessons and the study of the British Constitution, Sociology and Economics syllabuses for public examination did find a place not uncommonly in grammar schools and in the academic streams of comprehensive schools during the 1960s and 1970s.

Also in the 1960s community service programmes in schools (Groves, 1983) developed initially in the grammar and public schools. The Newsom Report (DES, 1963) emphasized the value to the young volunteer of involvement in community service and the subject began to appear not only as an extra-curricular activity but also as a time-tabled programme. It was commonly an option in the Sixth Form, an alternative to Physical Education for senior years and more often open (indeed sometimes obligatory) for low-achieving pupils in their last years of compulsory schooling. The raising of the school leaving age to 16 gave impetus to this development. Thus there has been a shift from community service existing largely for the intellectually able in schools to the opposite being true.

Outstanding examples exist, among which is Sevenoaks in Kent, where the Voluntary Service Unit coordinates a programme begun in 1973 'building from school to beyond school' (Groves, 1983).

In Cambridgeshire the LEA commissioned a review and evaluation of some programmes of community study/service in 1977. The researcher, P. Scrimshaw, later included much of this work in a broader work on *Community Service, Social Education and the Curriculum* (Scrimshaw, 1981). This work contains more analysis than elsewhere of the place of community service in the curriculum, the development of programmes of different types and some predictions and proposals for future policy. Scrimshaw prophetically anticipates a greater centre-periphery control of the curriculum with a simultaneous rising pressure for local community involvement, from parents and governors in schools.

In Northamptonshire a study of community service in secondary schools analysed systems of organization and looked in some detail at provision in six urban comprehensive schools (Cross, 1986).

The Schools Council (1967) on the subject of community service, was suggesting the need for links with the curriculum; a coherent strategy for evaluation and 'participation for all is still lacking'. 'Community service cannot achieve a fully effective place in Social Education until the issues are faced and objectives made clear'.

References to the more general idea of citizenship in the curriculum have been relatively rare but some are of interest: HMI (1977) were concerned that 'The 1980s may well be years of even greater political and economic tension, than the present day ... the greater will be the need for a basic political and economic education for all.'

DES (1980a) included in their suggested curriculum framework, in addition to core subjects, teaching leading to 'preparation for a participatory role in adult society' but did not specify any more detail.

In *A View of the Curriculm* (DES, 1980b), Proposition 12 is about personal and social development. Community studies and community service are mentioned with other aspects in a range of contexts in which personal and social development may be furthered.

In *Curriculum Matters 2* (HMI, 1985) there is reference to the need to prepare young people, within Personal and Social Education 'to contribute, co-operate and take the lead as appropriate within groups, to accept responsibility . . . schools might provide opportunities for social interaction, e.g. social functions and extra-curricular activities'.

> Schools need to examine what they provide intentionally as well as that which arises incidentally from the programme of work in order to ensure that pupils are given sufficient information and opportunity to use their initiative and to make informed choices; to exercise leadership and responsibility; to consider the consequences of their own actions and to develop positive moral qualities.

In *Better Schools* (DES, 1985) there is one reference to citizenship: 'some awareness of economic matters, notably the question of market forces, the factors governing the creation of private and public wealth, and taxation is a prerequisite for citizenship and employment'.

The National Curriculum (DES, 1987) makes no comment on any similar area of the curriculum. Rather it concentrates on the core subjects, and a later publication (DES, 1989a) mentions as cross-curricular issues careers, health, other aspects of social education and gender and multicultural issues. Themes running through the curriculum include economic awareness, political and international understanding and environmental concerns.

In *Curriculum Matters 14: Personal and Social Education from 5–16* (DES, 1989b) much advice is given to schools. Teaching approaches need to prepare school leavers for, among other experiences, those which they are about to encounter 'as young adults and citizens', social responsibilities include 'the rights and responsibilities of citizenship and decision-making in a democratic society'. Personal and social abilities and skills to be developed include how to 'take initiatives and act responsibly as an individual and member of the family, school or wider community'; and 'act as members of a democracy'.

Kenneth Baker, when Secretary of State for Education, made clear in July 1989 in the foreword to a CSV publication (Preecey and Marsh, 1989) that there is a great deal of work to be done in this area:

Schools should not see themselves in isolation from the community which they serve. Too often in the past schools have stood alone. The picture has changed in recent years, with closer contacts established with local groups and organisations. This is a healthy trend which the Government is actively promoting. The Education Reform Act stresses that the school curriculum should promote the moral and physical development of pupils and prepare them for the opportunities, responsibilities and experiences of adult life. By building into the curriculum properly planned and purposeful contacts between pupils and the community, schools can move towards these objectives and help to cultivate a sense of social responsibility in the young citizens of tomorrow.

It is a key aim of GCSE that examinations should test not only the recall of facts, but also whether pupils understand what they have been taught and can apply that knowledge to the everyday world. All GCSE syllabuses, as a condition of approval, encourage an awareness of relevant social, economic, political and environmental factors. That means highlighting the importance of qualities such as: self-reliance, self-discipline, a spirit of enterprise, a sense of social responsibility, and the ability to work harmoniously with others.

In October 1989 the National Curriculum Council gave some preliminary guidance to schools on the context of the National Curriculum in Circular No. 6 (NCC, 1989): 'The basic curriculum as described by law – the ten core and other foundation subjects of the National Curriculum plus Religious Education – is not intended to be the whole curriculum'. The circular describes cross-curricular provision under sub-headings – dimensions, skills and themes.

Citizenship (individual, family, community, national, European and international, including legal and political dimensions) is one of the cross-curricular themes. It is clear that schools will be expected to address the themes and co-ordinate links between different parts of the curriculum. They include a strong component of knowledge and understanding, in addition to skills. Most can be taught through other subjects as well as through other themes and topics. Some . . . may feature in PSE courses and all contribute to personal and social development in a number of ways.

The National Curriculum Guidance No. 3, (NCC, 1990a) published in March 1990 set out in more detail these expectations and outlined the dimensions, skills and themes and possible ways of managing their co-ordination and teaching in the whole curriculum. Curriculum Guidance No. 4 on 'Education for Economic and Industrial Understanding' (NCC, 1990b), No. 5 on 'Health Education' (NCC, 1990c),

No. 6 on 'Careers Education and Guidance' (NCC, 1990d), and No. 7 on 'Environmental Education' (NCC, 1990e) are documents which provide advice to schools on ways of moving forward with planning for a coordinated approach and managing its implementation. The eighth in the series is to provide similar guidance on citizenship as a cross-curricular theme and is imminent at the time of writing. Further titles will address equal opportunities and multicultural education, and skills: communication, numeracy, study, problem-solving, personal and social, and information technology.

Citizenship is definitely on the agenda of the school curriculum in the 1990s and debate about content, delivery, and implications, will clearly continue to be heard among pupils, teachers, parents, governors and members of the community around the school. There will be a variety of outcomes. The NCC does not lay down the methodology, but gives guidance on content and possible structures for delivery. The ethos of a particular school or college will have influence over the nature of provision.

Validation of pupils' activities, in school and outside, should be facilitated through the Record of Achievement (pupil profile) which has been becoming more common across the country in recent years. Nine pilot schemes were funded for three years (1985–8) by central government through the Education Support Grant (and there are currently some extensions to these). All were evaluated locally and there was a nationally coordinated evaluation report published in 1988 (Broadfoot *et al.*, 1988). Every education authority has been involved to a greater or lesser extent in development work. A 1990 deadline for all young people to take with them when they leave school a summary document recording achievement and negotiated teacher–pupil comment had been expected until August 1989, when it became clear that only National Curriculum assessment results would be required to be reported. In July 1990 good practice developing widely was commended:

> The government sees RoAs as integrally linked with the National Curriculum. The underlying principles of recognising achievement in all pupils are common to both . . . . For the future, we see RoAs as the means by which achievement across the National Curriculum and beyond can be most effectively reported to a range of audiences (DES, 1990)

Pupil participation

An important recommendation of *Improving Secondary Schools*

EA, 1984) was that pupils should be more involved in decision-making within their schools. They looked at 'pupil involvement and participation' in the schools they visited. In one school they found a two-tier system with both year and full school councils comprising student and staff members. They argue that such committee representation does give students a degree of power and responsibility as long as the issues raised for discussion go beyond the trivial and include the curriculum, assessment, extra-curricular activities and so on. They suggest that one way of giving purpose to schools' councils for pupils is to allocate a sum (say, £200) to be used by the council as they wish. This is an example of what is also true of movements in many other areas of the country to encourage pupil participation.

Whole school councils and year councils are very common. Eighty per cent of ILEA secondary schools (112 in number) responded to a survey (ILEA, 1988). Of these only 16 per cent said they had no form of pupil participation; 42 per cent had year councils and 31 per cent had whole school councils. Councils are generally felt to be beneficial for all involved and many of the schools not already having established them are in the process of setting them up. Councils discuss a wide range of issues including rules, social activities, discipline, curriculum, resources and administration.

Many schools now have pupil participation (as members or observers) in the governing body and parents and school associations. Tutorial discussion groups are often found to be a good way of giving pupils a chance to air their views. Teachers see the benefits of pupil participation as promoting competence, self-reliance, democracy and responsibility. There are problems associated with pupil participation and enthusiasm may wane if pupils do not achieve their objectives. 'Staff as well as pupils were disillusioned with pupil involvement, staff feeling frustrated when pupils did not utilise the opportunities afforded to them by the councils and when pupils did not follow their decisions through' (ILEA, 1988). Industrial action was reported to have disrupted pupil participation through the lack of teacher involvement out of school time.

> Whatever the organisation, school and year councils were generally felt to be of benefit to all aspects of the school. Pupils were said to acquire skills as well as a sense of involvement and responsibility. Teaching and support staff got to hear the pupils' point of view as well as benefiting from responsible involved pupils and many felt councils improved the teacher–pupil relationship. The school as a whole was felt to have a greater sense of community and cooperation, resulting in better working conditions for everyone.

The report highlights the need in future to look particularly at

- the number of black and working class pupils and girls involved in councils,
- the level of pupil involvement in the formulation and development of policy,
- pupils' perception of councils, their role, value and efficiency.

The experimental 'pupil parliament' in ILEA is worth mentioning in this context, though the development is too recent for any kind of evaluation. This initiative attempts to take pupil participation into LEA policy making. ILEA set up the country's first pupil parliament to give pupils a means of influencing decisions which shape the education they receive and can shape their lives. The parliament has so far met only once. Two hundred pupils gathered from all over London to debate their education. The particular issues which concerned them included: the new GCSE exam, teacher redeployment and ILEA's anti-racist and anti-sexist initiatives. The immediate question is, of course, whether such a so-called parliament would have any power. It might be beneficial in many ways, such as the development of debating skills, but without any real influence on schools it is not pupil participation. ILEA has said that this parliament's resolutions will go to the education committee, and some will be sent to schools and even, possibly, the Secretary of State. This is a development, then, which might involve pupils in a level of decision-making which has seldom been considered. (Swain, 1988)

Swain concludes his section on 'A say in management and planning' as follows:

From the available evidence . . . only a few general conclusions can be drawn.

(1) There are considerable outside pressures to limit democracy in schools. Watts, who was Head of Countesthorpe for a number of years, doubts whether an existing school could go over to a partici-patory approach of government.
(2) The school as a whole must be committed to participation as the starting assumption for all its decision-making. It helps too, if the school is backed by the LEA and school governors.
(3) Participation is not just a matter of schools' councils and committees. It must be reflected in the staff/student relationships, the organisation of groups, the organisation of time and the role of teachers.

It seems relatively easier to facilitate processes which give individual pupils more say in directing and controlling their own course of study. Indeed, recent developments of modular courses and 'negotiated

curriculum' may provide a basis for increased reflective pupil participation. In the light of evidence from studies of subject choice,
however, considerable attention is required in planning and evaluating
the processes of turning alternatives on paper into actual choices for
pupils (Swain, 1988).

The 1970s saw the growth of 'single issue politics', pressure groups and
protest groups; consumer groups, as well as protecting the rights of the
consumer, began to participate in the policy-making process; concern
grew about the apathy and low political awareness amongst the
electorate and future citizens; there were signs of increasing alienation
amongst young people and increased social, racial and political
tensions within urban communities.

These concerns prompted the Politics Association to conduct some
research, in 1975 (Stradling, 1975) into the political knowledge of
school leavers. The results illustrate the low political awareness of
young peole. Almost half the young people taking part in the survey
thought that the House of Commons makes all the important
decisions on the running of the country; 46 per cent could not name
even one pressure group; 25 per cent associated the policy of
nationalization with the Conservative Party; 44 per cent believed the
IRA was a Protestant organization.

In the 1980s there is still widespread political ignorance, apathy and
increasing political alienation. Many young people, particularly the
unemployed, feel excluded from the political process nationally and
locally.

> If people are to take a more active part in those political areas which
> have the greatest impact on their everyday lives and if they are to be
> more effective in making the bureaucratic system work for them, rather
> than for itself, they will need to learn not only how the system works,
> but how to influence it. This involves developing the political skills of
> organisation, persuasion, negotiation and participation. This raises
> important and controversial questions about the contribution of the
> educational system to their political development.
>
> Theories of participatory democracy therefore assign an important
> role to the educational system in general and the school in
> particular . . . which has the potential for providing opportunities for
> young people to practise the skills of democratic participation by being
> allowed to take part in the everyday running of the school.
>
> The school is in a unique position . . . since its primary function is to
> educate, it can provide opportunities for students not only to partici-
> pate but also to reflect on the intellectual, social and moral demands
> which genuine participation can make on them (Stradling, 1987).

Stradling offers the categories of: education *about* participation (which includes information about political issues, political institutions and decision-making processes); education *for* participation (which includes training to improve communication skills, political skills and concept development); and education *in* participation (which includes negotiating the curriculum, working on equal opportunities issues and moving towards greater democratic involvement of students in the running of the institution).

'Whilst lip-service is paid to school democracy there are very few concrete examples of democracy in action' (Stradling, 1987). Schools and colleges frequently have responsibilities which span the compulsory and voluntary involvement in education of their clients. There is seen to be a role for adult education to go out into the community and

> offer knowledge and expertise to those groups which are faced by political issues and problems but lack the skills, practical knowledge and political insight to mobilise effectively themselves or their resources to influence, block or change decisions and policies which directly affect them (Stradling, 1987).

Resource centres for community groups and other forms of community work aim to share what has been learnt about help and facilities with everyone who promotes community activity and demonstrate the advantages of supporting community development from a city or region-wide basis (Taylor, 1983).

Schools, and colleges then, are potentially the focus of much activity relevant to promoting the concept of citizenship:

- pupils may be involved in the discussion process (through year councils, whole school councils, representation on other bodies, tutorial programmes) which is influential in determining the way the school is run and developing participation and an understanding of the democratic process;
- pupils may be taught, through specialist courses (e.g. of PSE, current affairs, civics) or traditional subjects (e.g. History, Geography, Social Studies), about aspects of citizenship (e.g. the Legal System, Rights and Responsibilities, Political Education, Economic Awareness);
- schools may encourage pupils to take part in community service (through programmes in or out of school hours) so attempting to match need with assistance;
- adult education may be provided by community schools;
- the building in which the day school is housed may be a community centre where other groups which have a democratic or service interest (e.g. WI, environmental groups, Scouts, Playgroup, Lunch Club) meet;

- adults are involved in the running of the day school as volunteers (e.g. helping with classroom or library activities, accompanying trips, coaching sports teams);
- governing bodies and parent–teacher associations include many adults giving freely of their time to further the development of the school's activities.

Organizations involving young people in relevant activities

To give to young people an appropriate status as contributors to the community, some organizations choose to make no distinction on the basis of age. Rather, they prefer to be all-inclusive in their appeal. For example, International Voluntary Service, a movement founded in 1920, aims to promote international understanding and peace through bringing people together in work-camps for short periods of time and sending volunteers to work in developing countries. Activities are open to all over the age of 18; the great majority of participants are under 25. In 1988 they involved 920 volunteers in 61 work-camps – a commitment from volunteers of 100,000 volunteer-hours.

Despite this view, of including young people as of right in a general programme of volunteering, there exist a number of initiatives aimed specifically at young people. For example, in the late 1950s Voluntary Service Overseas began its work of enabling young people – principally pre-university entrants – to work in the developing countries for a year. Despite reported increasing difficulty in recruiting volunteers, recent figures show 1151 volunteers in the field (VSO, 1987). These are now almost entirely qualified professionals. More doctors, midwives, English teachers and motor mechanics could be used. The term of duty is now usually longer than a year.

CSV (Community Service Volunteers) has been active since 1962. It shares a founder with VSO. The Annual Review 1986–7 announced the 40,000th volunteer's enrolment and an income of over £14 million. CSV works on the assumption that anyone can contribute as a volunteer, and tries to change perceptions about 'good' volunteers, for example, through its Homeless Volunteer Scheme or its Young Offenders Programme which involves young prisoners in voluntary work. Two schemes operate that involve disabled people. In the Independent Living scheme, volunteers work with severely disabled people, providing day-to-day intensive support. 'Able to Help' is a scheme to give disabled people the opportunity to be volunteers themselves, again with volunteer support. CSV runs projects on health promotion by neighbourhood volunteers; home health development;

it involves early retired people; and provides volunteers to other groups. Eighty per cent of their volunteers are under the age of 24. In earlier years volunteers came forward with little effort on CSV's part to find them; now more effort needs to be made to recruit. CSV's Volunteer Programme involves at any one time about 800 volunteers on 600 projects. The average length of stay is 28 weeks. A recent success for CSV was the exemption of its full-time volunteers from payment of the Community Charge. They are paid only expenses and pocket money. Annually around 2,000 young people work full-time as volunteers with CSV in Britain in a variety of roles. Its recruits are generally Sixth Form leavers but it also actively encourages wide participation and partnerships between state-funding and voluntary activity. CSV operates a national advice and resource service for schools from their headquarters in London; over 3000 teachers purchased material in 1987–88 (see CSV, 1987–88; Ball, 1985).

Also with its origin in the 1960s (1968) is the national Community Development Foundation (formerly Young Volunteer Force Foundation and Community Projects Foundation) which now focuses its work on community development. It offers fieldwork and consultancy in active partnership with a wide range of public bodies to bring fresh thinking to bear upon local problems in search of creative solutions. Its chief activities and expertise are:

- running local community development projects directly;
- design, management, evaluation and support of local projects;
- relations between public bodies and the voluntary sector;
- advice to public and private sector organizations on community involvement.

The organization aims to enable local people to identify their own problems and come up with solutions – it is therefore a facilitator of links and support. In the organization's own words: '(We) help people develop skills of collective self-reliance and participation in public decision making, and help local authorities and other agencies to respond effectively to community needs. CPF's brief is to contribute to policy and practice in major social issues' (CPF, 1987–88; 1989). In 1988 it had an income from grants of more than £1.5 million, mostly from the Home Office and local authorities. It employs more than 100 staff and in 1987–88 reported involvement with 13 projects around the country. It will become involved in these projects with professionals employed by other institutions and with members of local communities who may be unpaid.

The work of CPF in community development crosses the

boundaries of statutory bodies, local and national, and the private and voluntary sectors. In 1978 Wolfenden spoke confidently of the role of voluntary projects in relation to 'the consolidation' of the welfare state. He recalled that many people had predicted that the voluntary sector would be redundant once the welfare state had been established; he showed that it was by no means redundant, and argued that it would always have a role in pioneering new forms of provision which would then be taken on board by statutory authorities.

> We can no longer make this assumption...funders might look in particular for a combination of realism about the dangers of serving to mask decline in statutory services, with an ability to use the new conditions creatively within the proper sphere of voluntary activity. Projects which appear to promise to mobilise voluntary labour to carry out functions of statutory authorities should be viewed with caution; the mark of genuineness in voluntary activity is the principle that the participants control their own purposes (Chanan, 1988).

The Council for Education in World Citizenship celebrated fifty years of existence in 1990. Its main aim, as its name makes clear, is to promote the study of world affairs in the education system of the United Kingdom. In promoting the concept of world citizenship many of its objectives focus on education for participation and responsible action. Its council has wide representation from organizations and its vice presidents include many eminent figures from public life, and members of parliament from both sides of the house. The 1987–88 Annual report lists 130 school meetings at which speakers covered subjects such as the work of an MP, the work of the Trade Union movement, media censorship, penal reform and environmental issues. Over 2000 schools and colleges are affiliated to CEWC – 80 per cent through LEAs. There are regular mailings of newsletters and broadsheets on current topics. The organization offers help with materials and curriculum development. National and local conferences are organized on such subjects as human rights, water, and citizens of Europe. There is a particularly active district council in Northern Ireland. CEWC has a small staff in London and volunteers in many parts of the country. It is financed by the DES (through the Central Bureau), subscription and donations, and is a registered educational charity.

The Politics Association has existed for nearly twenty years with the 'aim of fostering an informal political awareness' among young people. Their 'commitment is to Liberal Democracy which ...flourishes best when people play their part in the roles of the polity'

(Jones, 1987). The organization holds it as a duty 'to attempt in any educationally sound and objective way to overcome . . . ignorance and thus to underpin the safety of our democracy'. They have expressed a strong view that there should be a place for social and political education in the National Curriculum, perhaps teaching Politics formally or more typically including Civic Education in Humanities, Social Studies or Personal and Social Education.

Young Volunteer organizations on a local basis grew up around the country. They became coordinated in the *Young Volunteer Resource Unit* at the National Youth Bureau from 1974. Young Volunteer and Youth Action agencies are locally managed and locally funded voluntary organizations providing a wide range of opportunities to encourage young people's involvement in the community. The age range involved is from 12 to 30 years, but by far the greatest activity lies in the 13–19 age group. In 1986, 42 voluntary agencies and 8 statutory bodies employing 106 staff reached about 5000 young people (Smith, 1986). The number of groups has been decreasing in recent years. These organizations stress the importance of the voluntary involvement of young people in their local communities, and the need for careful preparation of the volunteer and the client so that the experience of community service can be a learning one. They are involved in the activities identified in the Thompson report (DES, 1982) as ranging 'from simple benevolence to participatory action'. Young people should be free to 'discuss, decide and act upon their own needs and the needs of others' (Hope, 1985; see also Garrett, 1986; NYB and YVRU 1981; Oldfield, 1988).

The statutory youth service operates a no-membership policy; figures of young people involved are therefore hard to estimate. The Thompson Report (DES, 1982) received submissions by hundreds of organizations (local and national) and individuals. The report traced the development of community involvement through the two previous decades mentioning initiatives in schools, further education colleges, higher education and the Youth Service. Simultaneously, community service became an alternative to custodial treatment for young offenders and YOP and YTS schemes were developed to address the issue of unemployment.

> In this way the idea of community service, used mainly to mean an organised pattern of activity in which young people perform tasks which are of benefit to other members of the community has become widespread; and special merits are claimed for it as a form of social education particularly appropriate to the time (DES, 1982).

These activities are strongly endorsed by the report if they are voluntary, if training is provided for worker and volunteer, if the context encourages reflection, if the whole spectrum from benevolence to participatory action is covered and if young people are involved in planning and management.

The Thompson Report commissioned Q Search of London to carry out a survey of 650 14–19-year-olds to inform the Report (DES, 1983). Among the findings were:

> Sixty per cent of young people probably have some contact with the Youth Service at some time.
> Twenty-nine per cent were currently involved. (There is concern generally that the Youth Service does not reach a large enough proportion of young people. Levels may vary much from one area of the country to another).

The Youth Service in Leicestershire in a recent review (1987) included the results of a questionnaire survey of 520 young people in the 14–21 age group. Asked if they spent time in volunteering or community action only 28 said 'Yes'.

Students in further and higher education may well be omitted from household surveys, and have perhaps broken with youth clubs, school and other organizations of earlier affiliation. To what extent are they involved in voluntary activity? The Student Community Action Development Unit reports (SCADU, 1987) more than 15,000 students to be involved through more than 100 groups in FE and HE institutions across the country. Working groups of the SCA network committee (1989–90) include groups focusing upon anti-racist action, good practice in volunteering and disability access. The activities vary very much from one-off events to placing volunteers with other organizations and regular student-organized community activities. These include running social clubs for people with mental disabilities, working in womens' refuges and girls' nights in youth clubs and setting up a group home where students share their lives with people with learning difficulties. Involvement may range from a few hours once a year to as much as seven hours a week. Most of the students involved with SCA are in higher education, living away from home, and have come into contact with the organization through their Students' Union.

There are many organizations which include community service in their activities which do have clearer numerical information about their membership. Organizations for young people feature in the statistics published in *Social Trends* (Central Statistical Office, 1989) and these show that many organizations have been experiencing falling membership over the period 1971–87. The Guide and Scout Association has a combined membership of 1.2 million but this figure is falling. Many of the uniformed national voluntary youth organizations offer structured programmes in which 'service' is a key part. The range of activities encompassed under this heading has broadened in recent years and includes conservation, first aid, work with children, local controversial issues of relevance to the community. Community involvement is seen as 'a continuing state of mind', 'community involvement is never ending' (Oldfield, 1988). Other groups experiencing a decline in membership include the Boys' and Girls' Brigade, Sunday Schools and the Red Cross. Those named as having rising membership include Army Cadet and ATC, Young Farmers' Clubs, Earth Action, Youth Amnesty, and the Duke of Edinburgh Award Scheme. The scene is not static.

In 1988 the Duke of Edinburgh Award Scheme (1988) reported a slight decline in the number of operating units but the number of Awards gained is increasing and reached its highest total for eight years. The Samaritans is reported nationally to have more than 1000 teenage volunteers (The Times, 30 November 1987). Volunteer Bureaux recruit young people as well as adults. They report the percentage of young volunteers to be steady. A recent survey (NYB, 1987) which issued 320 questionnaires to bureaux nationally received 52 returns. The most common response when asked what percentage of recruits were young people was 10 per cent (from 15 bureaux) although some few reported much higher figures (e.g. 90 per cent from 3 bureaux, 30 per cent from 8 bureaux). Of the bureaux responding, half said two-thirds of their volunteers were unemployed people most commonly referred by Job Centres. Bureaux aim at the whole age range. Many have some contact with young peoples' organizations. Volunteer Bureaux in 1989 numbered more than 400. They exist to recruit, place and monitor the work of volunteers (National Association of Volunteer Bureaux, 1986). About 120,000 volunteers are placed annually. They are linked in a national organization now located at a head office in Birmingham. Many problems over funding are quoted, causing some closures. Their work is also discussed in the report of some research done in 1978 for the Volunteer Centre (Hatch, 1983). It seemed then that people recruited through volunteer bureaux were not typical of the population as a whole – they were younger, predominantly female and included a disproportionate number of 'white-collar workers'. Neither were they typical of voluntary workers as a whole, being much more likely to be young women seeking their first experience of voluntary work. A new national survey is currently being produced.

Conclusion

This review of individual organizations demonstrates a wealth of activity. It is not easy to estimate the extent to which young people nationally are involved in these activities. Q Search (DES, 1983), in the report referred to above, asked respondents about social concerns and involvement. It found that:

> 71 per cent thought helping the elderly was important but 12 per cent claimed to be involved;
> 66 per cent thought helping the handicapped was important but 7 per cent claimed to be involved;
> 58 per cent thought conserving the countryside to be important but 6 per cent claimed to be involved;
> 37 per cent thought helping OXFAM was important but 6 per cent claimed to be involved;
> Girls were more likely than boys to be involved.

The majority agreed it was important for young people to be involved in some activities designed to improve the life of the elderly and/or handicapped, to improve urban environments and preserve the use of rural localities. It seemed to be deemed to be more important for others than self, as less than 10 per cent claimed personal involvement in such activities. Despite the high level of expressed social concern there is scope for a substantial increase in levels of personal commitment and active involvement by young people.

References

Ball, M. (1985) *Work and the Future*. London: CSV.
Batho, G. (1990) 'The history of the teaching of civics and citizenship in English schools', *The Curriculum Journal*, 1,1:91–107.
Broadfoot, P. *et al.* (1988) *Records of Achievement: Report of the National Evaluation of Pilot Schemes*. London: HMSO.
Central Statistical Office (1989) *Social Trends, 19*. London: HMSO.
CPF (1987–88) *Annual Report*. London: CPF.
CPF (1989) *The Cutting Edge: 21 Years of CPF*. London: CPF.
CSV (1987–88) *Annual Review: People for People*. London: CSV.
Chanan, G. (1988) *Community Development and the Voluntary Sector*. Research and Policy Paper 3. London: CDF.

33

Cross, S. (1986) *Getting Out - A Study of Community Service in Secondary Schools*. London. CSV.

DES (1963) *Half our Future: A Report of the Central Advisory Council for Education (England)*. (The Newson Report). London: HMSO.

DES (1980a) *Framework for the Curriculum*. London: HMSO.

DES (1980b) *A View of the Curriculum*. London: HMSO.

DES (1982) *Experience and Participation*. Report of the Review Group on the Youth Service in England, Cmnd 8686 (The Thompson Report). London: HMSO.

DES (1983) *Young People in the 80s*. A survey commissioned by the Thompson Report. London: HMSO.

DES (1985) *Better Schools*. London: HMSO.

DES (1987) *The National Curriculum 5-16: A Consultation Document*. London: HMSO.

DES (1989a) *The National Curriculum, Policy to Practice*. London: HMSO.

DES (1989b) *Curriculum Matters 14: Personal and Social Education from 5-16*. London: HMSO.

DES (1990) *Records of Achievement*. Circular 8/90. London: HMSO.

Duke of Edinburgh Award Scheme (1988) *Annual Report*. London: DEAS.

Garrett, B. (1986) *Report of an Action Research Project*. Croydon: Croydon Guild of Voluntary Organisations.

Groves, M. (1983) *Sevenoaks VSU*. Sevenoaks: Voluntary Service Unit.

Hatch, S. (1983) *Volunteers: Patterns, Meanings and Motives*. Berkhamsted: Volunteer Centre, UK.

HMI (1977) *Curriculum 11-16*. London: HMSO.

HMI (1985) *Curriculum Matters: HMI Series 2. The Curriculum for 5-16*. London: HMSO.

Hope, P. (1985) *Young People and the Community*. A consultative paper on behalf of the Community Involvement Development Group. Leicester: NYB.

ILEA (1984) *Improving Secondary Schools - Report of the Committee on the Curriculum and Organisation of Secondary Schools*. London: ILEA.

ILEA (1988) *Pupil Participation in ILEA Secondary Schools*. ILEA Research and Statistics RS 1181/88. London: ILEA.

Jones, B. (1987) 'National Curriculum 5-16. A response by the Politics Association', *Grassroots*, 45:6-8.

NCC (1989) *Circular Number 6. The National Curriculum and Whole Curriculum Planning; Preliminary Guidance*. York: National Curriculum Council.

NCC (1990a) *Curriculum Guidancce No. 3: The Whole Curriculum*. York: National Curriculum Council.

NCC (1990b) *Curriculum Guidance No. 4: Education for Economic and Industrial Understanding*. York: National Curriculum Council.

NCC (1990c) *Curriculum Guidance No. 5: Health Education*. York: National Curriculum Council.

NCC (1990d) *Curriculum Guidance No. 6: Careers Education and Guidance*. York: National Curriculum Council.

NCC (1990e) *Curriculum Guidance No. 7: Environmental Education*. York: National Curriculum Council.

National Association of Volunteer Bureaux (1986) *Introducing Volunteer Bureaux*. Berkhamstead: Volunteer Centre, UK.

NYB (1987) *Young People – Unemployment – The Volunteer Option*. Leicester: NYB.

NYB and YVRU (1981) *Community Involvement by Young People. An Area Survey*. Leicester: NYB.

Oldfield, C. (1988) *Community Involvement – The Youth Service*. Youth Action Mailing No. 32. Leicester: NYB.

Preecey, R. and Marsh, J. (1989) *Community Links with GCSE*. London: CSV.

SCADU (1987) *Annual Report 1987–8*. London: SCADU.

Schools Council (1967) *Working Paper 17*. London: Schools Council.

Scrimshaw, P. (1981) *Community Service, Social Education and the Curriculum*. Sevenoaks: Hodder & Stoughton.

Smith, D. (1986) *Basic Facts about Youth Action and Young Volunteer Agencies*. Leicester: NYB.

Stradling, R. (1975) *The Political Awareness of the School Leaver*. London: Hansard Society/Politics Association.

Stradling, R. (1987) *Education for Democratic Citizenship*. Strasbourg Conference on Parliamentary Democracy. Strasbourg: Council of Europe.

Swain, J. (1988) 'Pupil participation: an overview', in Hall and Wooster (Eds) *Human Relations in Education 9*. Nottingham: University of Nottingham School of Education.

Taylor, M. (1983) *Resource Centres for Community Groups*. London: Community Projects Foundation.

VSO (1987) *Annual Review*. London: VSO.

CHAPTER 4

Citizenship in Secondary Schools: The National Picture

Ken Fogelman

Introduction

Although the proposal that citizenship should be taught in our schools has been particularly discussed in the last year or so, it is far from new, as is indicated in Chapter 3. Members of the Speaker's Commission were well aware that much was already taking place, and of specific projects in some areas. However no evidence was available on the general picture; on whether and how the concept of citizenship was interpreted and being put into practise in schools throughout the country.

Thus, early in its deliberations, the Commission decided to seek evidence on this question, and commissioned the University of Leicester School of Education and Social and Community Planning Research jointly to conduct a survey of citizenship in secondary schools throughout England and Wales. The survey was funded by Esso UK. Fieldwork was carried out in the Autumn term of 1989, and a first report prepared for the Commission and for a national conference held in Northampton in February, 1990.

That first account of the findings was subsequently published (Fogelman, 1990) as an appendix to the Commission's report. This chapter incorporates the findings reported there, but also takes the analysis further, in particular by examining how certain characteristics of the schools were associated with their different approaches to the topic.

Sample and questionnaire

The questionnaire was distributed to a random sample of 800 maintained secondary schools throughout England and Wales. It was returned, completed and in time to be included in the analysis, by a total of 455, a response rate of 57 per cent. Given the extremely tight timetable and the many other demands on schools this is a very satisfactory response, in itself indicating the high level of interest and enthusiasm for this topic in many schools.

The questionnaire contained four main sections. The first asked for background information about the school, and the answers confirm the general representativeness of the sample. For example, 84 per cent of responding schools were comprehensive and 85 per cent co-educational. Just under half contained pupils from age 11 through to 18, and one third 11 to 16.

The remainder of the questionnaire was designed to explore citizenship in schools as broadly as possible without imposing a restricting definition, and taking into account the several facets of citizenship identified by the Commission and in other chapters of this book. The detailed content will be apparent from the presentation of findings below, but broadly three main areas were covered:

(1) Students' involvement in community activities and service organized by the school.
(2) Teaching within the school on subjects, topics and issues concerned with community and citizenship.
(3) Pupil participation in the decision-making structures of the school. This can be said to represent only a small part of that aspect of citizenship which is reflected in the ethos and personal relationships of a school, but it was felt to be the part appropriate to a survey of this nature. Such more sensitive issues would be better explored in the qualitative research which was being carried out at the same time (see Chapter 5).

Community activities and service

For each year-group schools were offered a list of possible activities and asked to indicate those in which their students were involved. Results for two year-groups, 12–13-year-olds and 15–16-year-olds are summarized in Table 4.1. These two groups are selected as being reasonably typical of the contrast between the periods before and after GCSE options have been determined and courses embarked upon.

As can be seen there is a very small proportion of schools where no

Table 4.1 Proportions of schools with pupils involved in specified activities

Activity	12–13-year-olds	15–16-year-olds
	%	%
Visiting or helping people:		
• the elderly in their homes	15	40
• the elderly in hostels/hospitals	8	40
• people with disabilities	8	22
• ill people in hospitals	3	4
• people in other health care situations	1	11
• children in nursery or primary schools	5	24
Other work for voluntary or statutory services or bodies:		
• environmental projects	22	18
• fund raising for charity (organizing, taking part, *not* just giving money)	86	26
• clerical or office help	3	1
• catering	5	1
Other activities	3	2
No pupils in the year group participating in such activities	10	3

pupils were involved in some such activities – just one in ten for the 12–13-year-olds, and fewer than one in thirty for the 15–16-year-olds. For the younger children, by far the most popular activity is fund-raising (but it should be noted that this involved some activity beyond simply giving money). In fact, for 43 per cent of schools this was the only activity reported for this age group. For the older pupils, greater involvement in a wider range of activities is reported, with particular emphasis on working with the elderly, the disabled and young children.

That the major change in activities occurs at the onset of GCSE courses is confirmed by further analysis. The proportion of schools with pupils involved in the range of activities other than fund-raising is about 50 per cent for each of the first three years and rises to about 85 per cent at 14–15 and 15–16. Furthermore, it remains at this level for 16–17-year-olds in the first Sixth Form year, but drops to around 70 per cent in the second year Sixth. Similarly the proportion with no pupils involved in any activities is around 10 per cent from 11 through to 14, 3–4 per cent from 14–17 and increases slightly to 8 per cent for 17–18-year-olds.

It seems likely that schools might vary in the opportunities for such activities which they offer according to, for example, where they are or the nature of their intake. In all, six school variables have been examined for whether they are related to any variation: school type (comprehensive, secondary modern or grammar); size; level of GCSE results in the previous year; proportion of ethnic minority pupils; catchment area (inner-city, suburban, small/country town or rural); and whether co-educational or single sex.

In general, any variation in relation to the first five of these school factors was small. There were no marked or consistent differences associated with the proportion of ethnic minority children in the school. There was some evidence of larger schools being able to offer a slightly greater variety of activities, with the highest reported levels of working with people with disabilities, in other health care situations and on environmental projects. Compared with other kinds of catchment area, more rural schools reported more involvement in visiting the elderly and working with younger children, but also the lowest levels of working with people with disabilities. Students in inner-city schools were relatively less often involved in visiting the elderly in their homes. Secondary modern schools reported slightly less hospital visiting and environmental projects, while grammar schools provided fewer examples of clerical and office work. The only contrast associated with the school's examination performance entailed less working with young children and fewer environmental projects in schools with the highest levels of results.

However, these differences were not dramatic and should be seen as no more than suggestive. The school factor which did reveal some more marked contrasts was whether the school was co-educational or single sex. This is shown in Table 4.2. For simplicity's sake, this is based on two year-groups combined to give the results for 14–16-year-olds, and categories of activities have also been combined.

There are of course relatively few single sex schools in the country, and they were relatively rare in the survey. Nevertheless, despite small numbers, several of the differences in Table 4.2 are highly significant statistically. Some of them could be attributed to fairly obvious gender stereotyping (whether on the part of the schools or their students we cannot comment). Boys' schools' involvement is substantially lower in each of: working with the elderly (chi square = 14.72, p < .001), health care (chi square = 11.82, p < .01); and working with younger children (chi square = 40.92, p < .001). Less predictably, boys' schools also report lower levels of involvement in environmental projects, although this difference does not reach statistical significance (chi square = 3.62). Overall, but excluding fund raising, the proportion of

Table 4.2 Community activities by school gender mix
(14–16-year-olds)

Activity	Co-ed Schools (n = 380) %	Boys' Schools (n = 28) %	Girls' Schools (n = 37) %
With the elderly	67	32	70
Other health care	65	32	62
With younger children	75	18	76
Environmental	43	25	46
Other, non fund raising	54	14	54
Any of the above	95	46	97
Fund raising	90	79	95
None participating in such activities	2	7	0

boys' schools saying that any of their 14–16-year-olds take part in any of these community activities is lower than half that of co-educational or girls' schools.

It is important to note that this survey was not designed to examine the experiences of individual children within these schools. It may seem unlikely, but it cannot necessarily be assumed, that such gender differences are not also present in the individual experiences of the pupils of co-educational schools.

The figures presented so far tell us only that some pupils were involved in these activities, not how many nor how regularly. These two issues were addressed in the next two questions. For 12–13-year-olds, one third (33 per cent) of the schools with some involvement reported that all or nearly all of their pupils participated in these activities. A further 24 per cent said that more than half did so, and in only 18 per cent was the proportion a quarter or fewer. For 15–16-year-olds the comparable figures were 29 per cent all or nearly all; 17 per cent more than half; and 36 per cent a quarter or fewer.

These levels of participation did not vary greatly in relation to the school characteristics. Schools in rural areas were somewhat more likely to report all or nearly all of their pupils involved, as also were secondary modern schools – and grammar schools had the lowest levels. Again, the major contrast concerned the single-sex schools. For example, 42 per cent of girls' schools said that all or nearly all of their 15–16-year-olds took part, as against 25 per cent of co-educational schools and only 14 per cent of boys' schools.

A further indication of the greater activity of older pupils is that just

12 per cent of schools with some participation reported that the involvement of most of their 15–16-year-olds was on just one or two occasions, whereas 29 per cent reported regular participation over a term or more (the remainder falling between these two extremes). For 12–13-year-olds the figures were almost reversed, with 10 per cent of schools claiming most of their pupils were involved regularly for at least a term, and 29 per cent saying that this was on only one or two occasions.

The figures for 12–13-year-olds showed little relationship with the school characteristics, although participation was a little less regular in schools in small towns and rural areas. The same was true for the 15–16-year-olds, and in addition secondary modern pupils were more likely to be regularly involved over a term or more, and grammar school pupils on only one or two occasions.

Not surprisingly, given their different position in relation to formal examination preparation, the way in which these activities were organized differed markedly between the two age groups. Although for both, about one in five of the schools indicated that these activities took place out of school hours, for the younger students only 5 per cent said that these activities took place within main curriculum subject lessons, whereas 34 per cent did so for the older students. For the 15–16-year-olds, 26 per cent of schools stated that these activities took place within a work experience placement.

Variation related to school characteristics mainly concerned older pupils and the extent to which activities were placed in main curriculum subjects and within school hours. Grammar schools, boys' schools and schools with high examination results all reported that activities were more likely to take place outside normal school hours.

A question of major interest to the Commission, and related to recent developments in assessment in many schools, concerns whether and how community activities by young people at school should be rewarded and recognized. It is not very long ago that it seemed that this would be part of a national records of achievement scheme. Although it is now clear that the statutory element in records of achievement will be limited to National Curriculum assessment, many schools and authorities are committed to wider-ranging schemes. This is reflected in Table 4.3, which also shows the many other ways in which student participation in community activity is currently recognized. Schools were asked to identify all methods which they used, so the figures in the Table add to more than 100 per cent.

For the younger age group, informal methods predominate, with

Table 4.3 Methods of reporting on and assessing community activity

Activity	12–13-year-olds	15–16-year-olds
	%	%
Community activity not reported on or assessed	13	7
Contributes to public exam	0	29
Part of other formal award scheme (Scouts, Duke of Edinburgh, etc.)	2	26
Contributes to record of achievement scheme:		
• self-assessment report	21	49
• teacher-assessment report	12	41
Other reports to parents	13	27
References for employers	1	63
Applications or references for higher or further education	1	38
Items in school assembly	49	53
Items in press, school magazine	47	59
Other	2	4

almost half of schools mentioning items in assembly, the press or the school magazine. Although no other one method is mentioned very frequently, only 13 per cent of schools state that community activities are not reported on or assessed at all for this age group.

It is clear that more formal assessment of such activities is much more common for the 15–16-year-olds. Items in assemblies and the press, etc. are still mentioned by more than half of the schools, but for more than a quarter these activities contribute to public exams or some other formal award. Most frequently reported is references to employers (68 per cent). That the figure for inclusion in references to higher or further education is somewhat lower (38 per cent) may simply reflect that this is less appropriate for this age group. Among schools with 17–18–year-olds involved in community activities, 60 per cent said that these were reported in such references.

Citizenship studies within the school

The next section of the questionnaire was concerned with the place of citizenship within the school's curriculum. Schools were asked to report on 'subjects, topics or issues concerned with community and citizenship that can be broadly defined as political, civil and social rights and duties'.

Some insight into the importance which a school places on this area of the curriculum can be inferred from how it is managed within the policy and management structure of the school. Forty-three per cent of schools reported that they had an agreed policy or curriculum document or written statement particularly about citizenship studies within the school, although for only 5 per cent was this a separate document rather than part of some wider curriculum document.

Table 4.4 shows that there are some major differences according to school characteristics in this respect. To some extent these reflect similar differences of emphasis to those we have already seen in relation to community activities. Grammar schools, boys' schools and schools with high examination results are less likely to have a policy or curriculum document on citizenship. Also notable is the relatively low figure for schools with a higher proportion of ethnic minority pupils.

Schools also varied in where responsibility for citizenship within the curriculum was placed. Twenty-one per cent stated that it was co-ordinated or overseen by a member of the school's senior management team, and in a further 18 per cent some other member of staff had a

Table 4.4 Agreed policy or curriculum document by school characteristics

	% Yes
Comprehensive	44
Secondary Modern	46
Grammar	21
Co-educational	45
Boys'	29
Girls'	37
Size:	
−700	48
700–899	43
900+	38
Percentage 5+ A–C GCSEs in previous year:	
−15	42
16–25	50
25–40	48
40+	33
Percentage ethnic minority pupils:	
−1	44
1–10	48
10+	30
Inner-city	44
Suburban	47
Small/country town	42
Rural	43

specific responsibility for this area. In the remainder, implementation depended on the initiatives of particular departments or teachers. Dependence on individual initiative was more likely in grammar and secondary modern schools than comprehensives. Perhaps unsurprisingly, it was in the largest schools that responsibility was likely to rest with a specific member of staff who was not a member of the senior management team.

One of the most important areas about which questions were asked concerned the actual topics taught in the schools which they considered to be relevant to citizenship. However, this has proved also to be a more difficult area on which to present results, because of the great variety of topics identified. They cannot be systematically summarized, but the examples below may help to give a flavour of that variety:

12–13-year-olds –

> nature conservation; charity involvement; pollution; the Christian community; support for the Third World; health and safety; the family; relationships; making choices; voting and the parliamentary system; police and policing; the aged; alcohol education; eating for health; recreation; smoking; skills for adolescence; people who serve our community; Third World communities; personal safety; decision-making; lifestyles; money management.

15–16-year-olds –

> world of work; health morals; conflict and reconciliation in the community; national and international affairs; trade unions; duties and rights of adults; family responsibility; social awareness; the media; the school and the community; mental health studies; sexual relationships and decision-making; persecution and prejudice; using local agencies; body abuse; local government; parliament; child care; crime and crime prevention; consumer awareness; population growth; care of elderly people; handicap in the community; respect for the environment; child development; youth cultures.

Correspondingly, there is variety in the subject areas within which these topics are covered by schools. When asked to identify all the relevant subject areas in which they were taught, as many as 11 per cent indicated that they taught Citizenship as a separate subject within the curriculum. More frequently it was included in more familiar subject areas such as History, Geography and Humanities (78 per cent), Home Economics (62 per cent), English (60 per cent), Business Studies (45 per cent), Economics (28 per cent) and Social Studies (28 per cent).

Also frequently mentioned as areas in which aspects of citizenship were covered were CPVE (Certificate of Pre-vocational Education) courses (37 per cent) and BTEC Foundation Studies (24 per cent). In addition, 77 per cent reported that some aspects were covered in form time or tutorial groups. However, most frequently mentioned of all was PSE (Personal and Social Education), by 95 per cent of schools. When then asked to identify the *one* subject area within which most citizenship studies teaching took place for *most* pupils, PSE was by far the most frequently selected by schools (67 per cent). The only other subject areas mentioned by significant numbers were form time (15 per cent) and Humanities (9 per cent). Only 1 per cent (i.e., 4 schools) indicated that Citizenship as a separate subject was their main method.

As might be expected, larger schools appear better able to offer a greater range of curriculum options. They more often provided Citizenship as a separate subject, but also more frequently reported that aspects were covered in Economics, Politics, Home Economics, Social Studies, CPVE and BTEC. No doubt for different reasons, grammar schools, schools with high examination results and schools in suburban areas were also most likely to indicate coverage in Economics and Politics lessons.

A specific question was put to the schools on the amount of classroom time which was spent on Citizenship and Community Studies. Table 4.5 summarizes their responses for the two selected age groups.

The Table suggests substantial variation among schools, but for both age groups the most common situation is of regular lessons throughout the year. The figures for the older students are a little difficult to interpret as, not surprisingly at this stage, more than a quarter of the schools stated that classroom time varied according to subject options. Nevertheless, it is noteworthy that only 2 per cent of

Table 4.5 Amount of classroom time spent on Citizenship/Community Studies

	12–13-year-olds	15–16-year-olds
	%	%
None	14	2
1–5 lessons a year	24	10
Regular (at least once a week) lessons for half a term	7	8
Regular lessons for one term	4	4
Regular lessons for two terms	1	2
Regular lessons through the year	43	46
Varies according to subject options	6	27

schools reported no classroom time at all for the subject with this age group, compared with 14 per cent at age 12 to 13.

Perhaps because of the nature of the links with specific subjects described above, grammar schools were more likely to have regular lessons over the year for older children, but less likely to follow this pattern with the younger group than comprehensives or secondary moderns. Otherwise the patterns of lessons did not vary according to the school characteristics.

Pupil representation

Many teachers would argue that, in preparing young people to take their place as adult citizens, the general ethos of the school, as exemplified by relationships between staff and students and pupils' involvement in decisions, are at least as important as what is taught or experiences of community activity. A more sensitive exploration of these areas was beyond the scope of this survey, but the opportunity was taken to ask about pupil representation and participation in a number of respects. The answers to these questions are summarized below:

		%
(1)	schools which organize mock (political) elections	54
(2)	schools which have a school council or year or house councils, on which pupils are represented	60
(3)	those with a school council, etc., for which pupil members are elected by the student body	97
(4)	those with a school council, etc., on which all year groups are represented on the council(s)	70
(5)	schools with pupil representation at meetings of the school governors:	
	regularly	13
	sometimes	8
(6)	schools with pupil representation at meetings of the PTA or equivalent body:	
	regularly	9
	sometimes	14
(7)	schools with pupil representation on any other body or committee	25

The other bodies or committees described under (7) were very varied. Several schools referred to a prefects' or Sixth Form committee. Among other examples given were: charity committee; local crime prevention panel; police advisory committee; local schools' consortium; marketing group; farm management group; book

Table 4.6 Pupil representation by school characteristics

	Mock elections	School council	Pupils at governors' meetings	Pupils at PTA meetings
Comprehensive	55	63	22	23
Secondary Modern	36	39	4	14
Grammar	74	58	5	37
Co-educational	55	61	19	22
Boys'	57	36	21	11
Girls'	45	68	32	40
Size:				
− 700	49	55	18	25
700–899	55	58	19	23
900 +	59	67	25	21
Percentage 5 + A–C GCSEs in previous year:				
− 15	44	57	29	21
16–25	47	55	22	28
25–40	60	65	21	26
40 +	64	61	15	19
Percentage ethnic minority pupils:				
− 1	56	60	15	21
1 – 10	55	52	18	27
10 +	47	75	39	24
Inner-city	38	63	31	28
Suburban	54	61	23	22
Small/country town	64	57	13	21
Rural	63	70	17	30

committee; Soviet exchange committee; school mini-bus appeal committee; action group to fight school closure.

The major ways in which schools' responses to the questions on representation varied according to their characteristics are indicated in Table 4.6.

There are many interesting differences in Table 4.6, but the most notable relate to the selectivity and sex of the school. Secondary modern schools have the lowest proportions on each of the four indicators of pupil representation. This may suggest that it is older pupils who take part in such activities, but the low proportion of grammar schools with pupils present at governors' meetings implies that it may also be an indication of philosophy.

Single-sex boys' schools are least likely to have a school council or pupils at PTA meetings, whereas these and representation at governors' meetings are more frequently reported by girls' schools. On the other hand, girls' schools are least likely to have held mock elections.

Also worthy of comment is the high proportion of schools with relatively large numbers of ethnic minority pupils having a school council and pupils at governors' meetings, but the lower proportion holding mock elections.

Conclusions

In general, the survey has confirmed that many schools have elaborate programs related to citizenship both in terms of community service and within the more formal curriculum; and very few indeed say they are doing nothing. However, the extent and nature of this provision is clearly very variable from one school to another – and within schools as far as the experiences of individual pupils are concerned. Although many of the approaches and activities identified by the National Curriculum Council and the Speaker's Commission are already to be found in schools, it is apparent that provision is often patchy, dependent on the initiative of individual teachers, and probably often available to only particular sub-groups of pupils.

The findings point to a number of specific issues. One concerns the experiences of different age groups. Fund raising is a commendable activity, but it is not clear why this should be the major, or even sole, focus of contribution to the community for children up to the age of 14. This survey has concentrated on the secondary phase. Would we find the paucity of other activities in primary schools implied by extrapolation of these results? Or is it that secondary schools under-estimate what their younger students could do and fail to build upon their experiences towards the top end of primary schooling? Equally, the fact that for older pupils many aspects of citizenship are addressed within specific subjects, in PSE and in activities related to work experience, identifies the need for careful monitoring to ensure that each pupil receives an integrated set of topics and experiences, without major gaps or duplication.

The role of specific subjects also touches upon the different experiences of pupils of different ability. Although this was not examined directly, the fact that grammar schools and others with the highest examination results were, for example, more likely to provide their community activities outside school hours, less likely to have a policy or curriculum document on citizenship, and more likely to place their teaching of citizenship within subjects such as Economics or Politics – not subjects taken by large numbers – suggests lower priority may be given to citizenship experiences for more able children.

There is a strong suggestion of some gender stereotyping. Boys' schools were particularly unlikely to involve their pupils in a range of community activities, including those with the elderly, the disabled and younger children. Although co-educational schools as a whole were as likely as girls' schools to have some pupils involved in such activities, the latter involved more of their pupils, which may suggest some gender differences within co-educational schools. There are other suggestions of a less advanced commitment to the concepts underlying citizenship among boys' schools – they were, for example, less likely to have a policy or curriculum document, or a school council.

Although there are several issues which schools will need to address, there is nothing in these results which should lead to criticism of their response to date. The survey took place only a few months after Citizenship had been identified as a cross-curricular theme, and there is clearly a substantial base of activity on which to build. The challenge is to ensure that all the nation's children receive relevant, well-planned and coherent experiences over the totality of their school years.

Reference

Fogelman, K. (1990) 'Citizenship in secondary schools: a national survey', Appendix E, in Commission on Citizenship, *Encouraging Citizenship*. London: HMSO.

CHAPTER 5

Approaches to Citizenship

Meriel Vlaeminke and Max Burkimsher

Introduction

This chapter draws on the findings of a survey of 26 secondary schools in Leicestershire and Northamptonshire conducted between October 1989 and February 1990. The schools had all indicated their commitment to promoting the notion of citizenship amongst their students and they represent a variety of catchment areas, size and age range (from 9 years upwards) and included three single-sex schools and one special school.

The first stage of the survey involved interviews with heads and/or deputies as well as colleagues with a designated responsibility in some area of citizenship. The aim was to obtain an overview of each school's approach to the concept of citizenship – to identify those areas to which schools attach particular importance. The second stage consisted of longer visits to 12 of the schools in order to talk to a wider range of personnel – pupils, teachers, governors, parents and other members of the community – and to observe in practice some of the activities and special events identified by the schools as relevant to citizenship education.

What is presented in the following pages is the collective view of the schools in the survey. The researchers were concerned to ascertain how citizenship is perceived in this group of interested institutions, and to present their ideas and practices in the form of a descriptive summary. Whilst a degree of interpretation is implicit in our organization of the copious and varied material we collected, we have been committed throughout to voicing accurately the schools' view rather than to evaluating, judging and comparing.

All schools acknowledged the importance of preparing pupils for citizenship, though the term was not generally in use until very recently. They saw this preparation as taking place

(1)   through the ethos of the school
(2)   through the organizational structures of the school
(3)   in a wide variety of locations within the curriculum as well as in extra-curricular and non-school activities
(4)   by means of appropriate forms of recognition and assessment.

These four headings afford a structure for the chapter, while recognising that none is discrete or unrelated to the other three.

Ethos

The ethos – or atmosphere or climate or spirit – of institutions both controls and derives from all the practices that go on within them. It does not have a separate existence, yet its particular identity will infuse all other aspects of life and be unique to each school community.

Education for citizenship is founded on the quality of relationships and respect for individuals, and involves perceptions of justice, fairness, freedom and rights. It implies acceptance of a set of values which can be shared, to enable a disparate group of people to work as a happy and purposeful community. It requires the provision of contexts for the development of positive attitudes about self and others through such means as opportunities for negotiation, teamwork, the exercise of responsibility, decision-making, experiential learning and pupil-centred approaches both in and out of the taught curriculum. None of this points to uniformity or standardization but rather to an underlying consistency which should permeate the varied experiences of each member of a school's community.

Of the utmost importance is striving for consistency in all the relationships in which a pupil is involved. As schools become more open to 'outsiders' and more engaged with their communities, pupils are being expected to relate to a much more diverse collection of people, some of whom are taking on direct responsibility for a part of their education. It is essential, therefore, that all concerned should be sympathetic to the aims of the school and the ethos which it is trying to create; the alternative can only be detrimental to both individual pupils and the school. Some schools recognize that routine everyday contacts between staff and pupils do not always match up to the higher ideals embodied in special projects or enterprises where the qualities associated with good relationships are specifically targeted for emulation. The implications for a whole-school approach, involving everyone, are clear.

Education for citizenship is also about empowerment and access. Pupils can only learn about the exercise of rights and responsibilities if afforded practical opportunities to do so – and those opportunities need to be varied, progressive and relatively safe. A genuine commitment to this principle manifests itself in numerous ways in the life of a school, from the adoption of pupil–centred approaches in the classroom, to opportunities for initiatives from interest groups, tutor groups and the like, to major organizational enterprises in which the pupils are encouraged to play a full part. We came across some impressive examples of pupils, sometimes quite young, taking on considerable responsibilities – organizational, decision-making, financial – while the schools played a supportive, facilitating role.

School councils provide a formal mechanism for the participation of pupils in the development of the school. Most head teachers spoke of the importance of according real status to the council, of encouraging members to research their proposals and present their case, and of being seen to take up some of the council's suggestions. They acknowledged the range of learning experiences inherent in pupil involvement with this exercise of democracy, such as familiarity with the protocol of formal meetings and with agendas and minutes; communication skills; some understanding of power relations, decision-making and financial constraints; and recognition of the importance of consultation, compromise, boundaries and justice.

Among the features which seem to make for a successful school council are a written constitution; a schedule of meetings in school time; attendance by senior members of staff (often the head); structures for ensuring widespread participation in generating agendas and supplying feedback; and control of a small budget. At council meetings, pupils were observed to speak succinctly and without rancour, and to show awareness of the complexities of issues, the consequences of decisions and the interests of others, especially younger members of the council.

Two key factors in creating the desired ethos are the ways in which a school articulates its requirements regarding pupil behaviour and then deals with behaviour which fails to meet its requirements, i.e., rules and sanctions. Some schools have involved pupils fully in devising codes of conduct or policies on particular issues, e.g., bullying and graffiti. Others see it as important to limit written rules to a few simple principles which are understood to cover the details of everyday life and thereby aim to encourage a sense of personal responsibility.

Discussion, counselling, placing on report and parental involvement are virtually universal ways of dealing with unsatisfactory behaviour. This approach is regarded as a key element in the personal development of pupils, alongside the provision, whenever possible, of opportunities for such pupils to enjoy a positive experience of schooling. The aim in this part of school life is to work towards the shared values referred to earlier, while also explaining the expectations and constraints regarding behaviour in any community which is to function successfully.

Crucial to achieving the goals of individual self-esteem and respect for others is an effective policy of equal opportunities. All schools acknowledge the importance of this aspect of education for citizenship and a number have positive and imaginative programmes in place. These more commonly relate to multicultural and anti-racist policies and to the integration of children with special needs than to inequalities arising from gender differentiation.

To quote from the directly-worded opening page of one school's brochure:

> – School deplores discrimination of any kind on grounds of colour, race, religion, sex or disability, and aims to promote equal opportunities for all . . . . This school is opposed to any form of racialist activity and will take appropriate action to deal with any incidents which arise.

Schools with a significant proportion of pupils from ethnic minorities naturally draw on the resources of the pupils themselves. In one 11–14 institution, for instance, a language awareness project is used as the basis for field work in the local community and for anti-racist work in school. Where there are few pupils from ethnic minorities, schools look to a wider range of resources to enhance understanding of culture and race. Examples include a study of Jewish communities and customs, practical workshops run by the LEA's multicultural team, and the offering of community languages within the modern language framework.

Contact with youngsters (and adults) with special needs is widely used as part of schools' community service arrangements and increasingly as a learning experience to develop awareness and understanding. In this context, the maturity and compassion with which several groups of pupils were seen to approach some quite challenging situations were worthy of note. Helping at a psychiatric hospital, working alongside children with mental handicaps in school, assisting with swimming, horse-riding and other activities in a special school, all invoked responsible, caring and good-humoured attitudes which the staff believed made an invaluable contribution to their pupils' education.

The differing experiences of schooling among girls and boys is seen as a cause for concern but progress seems to be slow. Most schools include units on women's rights (or similar) within the curriculum and there are marginal shifts in the taking of non-traditional subjects by both sexes. Some fruitful projects in CDT, such as designing a bed-sitting room or making toys for young children, serve to engage girls and boys in 'new' areas of learning and offer opportunities for both sexes to excel. But options like child care or parentcraft, where they still exist, are almost exclusively female and it is not easy to find ways of challenging stereotypical attitudes to adult roles and gender-typed behaviour.

It is impossible to arrive at rules or guidelines to define 'ethos'; it must always be an organic part of an institution, and the people working within it. However, two styles of development can be identified. In one a clearly defined philosophical base is established and all the school's structures and activities are planned to flow therefrom. Commitment to the concepts of democratic schooling or the just community are examples of such an approach. In the other, bolt-on or individual initiatives which flourish and are seen to have an impact on the quality of educational experience, become absorbed into the school organism and thereby influence its ethos. Sometimes the personal enthusiasm of one individual can begin to affect the priorities, organization and curriculum of a school until it pervades its whole atmosphere and ethos.

Organization

If the ethos of the school is a crucial part of education for citizenship, it goes without saying that the staff individually and collectively must be seen to accept and contribute to the same ethos. This is no less true of the organization as a whole. Inconsistency at any point will at best be a source of difficulty and at worst be seen as hypocritical. Furthermore, if schools see themselves as communities in which all members have a part to play, it is important that organizational structures should provide opportunities for and encourage the involvement of all. To this end, management teams involve staff in consultative and participative roles which enable individuals to use initiative and thereby engender a sense of ownership of the schools' development. Thus a corporate or collegial rather than an hierarchical style of operation is favoured.

Education for citizenship, viewed broadly as preparation for adult life, requires education to be seen in an holistic way. The traditional organization of secondary schools (in contrast to primary and many middle schools) into quasi-autonomous subject departments is a structure with considerable limitations in this respect. Many schools, therefore, are actively seeking ways to circumvent this difficulty and provide for better coordination across the curriculum.

A faculty structure is identified as one way of effecting this in schools with older pupils and some have grouped their departments into as few as three areas of learning experience. Faculty directors are likely to have a coordinating role within their own area and to be responsible for developing inter-faculty links. Some schools have established posts of responsibility for cross-curricular learning. The coordinators are often supported by teams of teachers providing direct links with each department or faculty. Such groups have been responsible for a number of curricular innovations.

The holistic view is also developed by drawing together academic and pastoral strands so that year or division heads are involved in the curricular experience of their students. This trend is supported by the enhanced role of the form tutor who monitors the students' progress and is frequently the first point of contact between parents and school. Tutors are also key figures in the process leading to records of achievement. This provides a context for tutor–student discussion which can play an important role in developing positive relationships and student self-esteem; for example, by noting the student's achievements in the field of community involvement.

A further role for management lies in the realm of the timetable. One consisting of many short periods is a straitjacket which hinders cross-curricular initiative. The normal pattern in the sample of schools was a four- or five-period day but with additional flexibility created by the use of occasional long-block timetabling. These longer periods of time, from half days to whole weeks, open up the opportunity for community-based activities or special assignments, often on cross-curricular themes, such as technology, industry, health, expressive arts and equal opportunities. One school provides week-long projects for each of its year groups, another sets aside one week per half term for longer assignments involving all faculties.

Teaching and learning

The common feature of all activities using longer time blocks is a dramatic shift away from didactic teaching to more varied forms of pupil-centred, active or experiential learning. Secondary schools are thus rediscovering the value of approaches which are the norm in primary and many middle schools. One difference lies in the scale of operations in secondary schools since it is common for whole year-groups (involving from 150–400 students) to be involved simultaneously on some activities.

The change in teaching and learning styles is seen to alter and improve the relationship between teacher and student. For students more emphasis is placed on cooperating in groups, research skills, problem-solving, negotiation and decision-making while the teacher becomes more of a facilitator. In other words, students take more responsibility for their own learning, an essential element in an ethos which helps to develop qualities for citizenship.

The development of such learning styles has also been fostered in recent years by a variety of other influences including active tutorial work, the Lower Attaining Pupils Project (LAPP), CPVE, TVEI, GCSE and BTEC/City and Guilds foundation courses. It is worth noting that many of the features of the LAPP have been taken up in TVEI and are now being extended to all students – for example, work experience, community service, residential experience, project work and records of achievement. All these activities were identified by schools as significant in education for citizenship.

While schools showed general agreement on these points, there were some major differences in the proportions of pupils and the age groups engaged on particular activities at each school. This points to the need to establish for all students an entitlement to a coherent, balanced programme of education for citizenship. In the past, secondary schools would have had difficulty in providing and monitoring such an entitlement through the sea of diversity created by many option systems. The framework of the National Curriculum perhaps provides an opportunity to find a way round this problem. To do this may well involve putting into effect the advice in *Curriculum Guidance 3* (NCC, 1989) to 'throw all the attainment targets in a heap on the floor and re-assemble them in a way which provides for them the very basis of a whole curriculum'.

Several schools have, in fact, built aspects of education for citizenship into their core curriculum. In one, for example, an English department plays an important role in the work experience programme to facilitate its use in meeting GCSE course-work requirements. In another, all year 9 and 10 students are able to obtain first aid and life-saving awards through PE, while a third has built modules of community service and child study in a GCSE in Humanities which is taken by all pupils.

However, although some aspects of citizenship fit readily into particular programmes of study, others appear as fragments in several subjects. There is a clear role here, widely recognized by the secondary schools, for separately timetabled PSE as a means of drawing these pieces together and at the same time engaging pupils in reflective thinking.

All schools spoke of fruitful links with industry and considerable enthusiasm was expressed for ventures in which industrialists actively worked with teachers to organize experience based in school. A flexible secondment was being used in one instance to provide staff with the time and opportunity to build such community involvement into the curriculum. School–industry–community liaison or support groups have developed industrial tutor schemes in which people from industry or the wider community act as tutors to small groups of students. For the tutor this provides an opportunity to learn from the students about current developments in education.

Industry days (and weeks) are well established. These vary in format but are likely to include simulations involving role play, team work, accounting and financial planning, labour relations, marketing strategies, competition, and environmental issues. The scale and contexts vary from local to world-wide, while some simulations incorporate international trade and world development issues. There are also opportunities for the development of information processing and foreign language skills.

Short modular courses provide a context within which some firms find it easier to contribute to the curriculum. By the same means community and university links can be built in; the latter a valuable way of opening the eyes of younger pupils from a variety of backgrounds to the possibilities of higher education.

Community placements or involvements are organized in all schools and an interesting and often imaginative variety of activities is taking place. Playgroups, special schools, luncheon clubs and old peoples' homes figure largely, and some students are involved with younger children in their own or other schools using their expertise in computing, in language work, etc. More unusual activities include: producing a regular radio programme for the blind; running a large print library; designing and making a stained glass window for a local church (an A-level Design project); designing and making toys for the blind; a working visit to the Gambia; producing a directory of voluntary agencies in the locality; working as tree wardens.

While all schools arrange community placements for some pupils, only a minority provide such experience for all, usually by means of a modular programme. Placements are used fully as educational experiences with careful preparation, self-assessment and evaluation, involving pupils, tutors and host organizations. Work experience is approached in a similar way.

In several schools with 9–13 or 11–14 age ranges, pupils have the opportunity for community placement, and further opportunities exist when these pupils move to upper schools or colleges. In 11–18 schools, community experience is normally concentrated in the senior age groups. It is important, therefore, to identify an appropriate progression of experience across phases, and perhaps also to appreciate the capabilities of relatively young pupils in tackling this type of activity.

Schools exercise great care in arranging placements, matching them with the needs and abilities of individual pupils and consulting with hosts. Such care and progression are exemplified in the programmes arranged for young people with learning difficulties.

The many schemes involving contact with children with disabilities were seen to bring out qualities of maturity and understanding in participants. In one school, pupils of all ages unobtrusively took trouble to ensure the involvement of the children with mental handicaps working alongside them; in others, 13–14 year olds assist a range of activities at special schools. Careful preparation and monitoring are crucial in such arrangements, but the rewards can be considerable. In one case, students reported an enormous sense of responsibility working with children with severe disabilities, and a much greater awareness of the needs of people who are often not obvious in the community. In another, resourcefulness and strength of character were cited as key qualities in helping children whose behaviour could be unpredictable. Asked about the value of her presence in a school for children with learning difficulties, one 13-year-old commented that she felt she was helping pupils to take responsibility for themselves. A number of the supervising staff spoke eloquently of the warm and caring attitudes – or, as one put it, 'the love' – shown by their pupils, who, they admitted, were more natural and competent in such situations than they themselves were.

In several schools there were projects where the visits of mainstream pupils were part of a careful process of preparation to enable reciprocal visits by pupils from special schools. Young pupils demonstrated keen insight into the consistency of attitudes towards the disabled. One commented, 'there is a need for a lot more interaction from an earlier age to break down barriers'.

Residential experience is an important social experience, into which many activities and forms of learning are incorporated. Considerable effort is put into overcoming family and financial difficulties in order to involve all children, even if only for a short period, by providing a range of experiences which are varied in appeal, in duration and in cost. Opportunities include field trips, group and individual exchanges, ski trips, tours, work experience, outdoor pursuits, or even, for one small group, an overnight stay on the school premises. The activities are as practical as possible and student involvement is maximized. Planning, personal organization, leadership, group and individual reponsibility, problem-solving, self-reliance, self-awareness, thinking for oneself and fitting in with others are all features of this type of exercise.

The effectiveness of any operation which involves suspending the normal timetable and makes extra demands on staff must be carefully evaluated, against pre-established criteria. The sharing of knowledge and experience between schools is of great value. To this end Northamptonshire has set up a support group of teachers and advisers to produce information and guidance on residential education.

In political education most schools aim to give their pupils an understanding of how democratic institutions function, through the processes involved in operating a school council, clubs or societies. Local councillors, Members of Parliament and Members of the European Parliament are invited, and one school reported a particularly successful session when, owing to the Mayor's sudden illness, the annual talk on civic affairs was given by the chauffeur!

A number of schools organize trips to the Houses of Parliament but places are usually limited, even though one undertakes to get all its pupils there at some time during their school career. An imaginative alternative in one school for a whole year-group involved Year 9 in a morning of varied activities including:

● a multi-choice quiz to open up the subject
● group discussions on issues relating to the vote and systems of representation

● an explanation of parliamentary conventions using a video of Prime Minister's question time
● simulated hustings in which classes were addressed by fellow pupils acting as parliamentary candidates
● polling and declaration of results.

The afternoon session was devoted to a parliamentary debate in which the whole year-group participated as 'MPs' in a hall set out to resemble the chamber of the House of Commons. At the conclusion a vote was taken with 'members' filing through appropriate lobbies.

Another special exercise involved a number of secondary schools in a simulation of the European Parliament. After a weekend's preparation at a local college, three-member 'delegations' from each Community country debated issues relating to sovereignty and the environment, in the council chambers in Northampton. Participants reported a raising of their awareness of the views of Community members, particularly smaller countries, and of issues such as the nature of bias and self-interest.

All schools expect to give their students – often through the Humanities curriculum – some introduction to broader political issues, such as human rights, the workings of trade unions and the role of pressure groups. This may well lead on to students initiating campaigns, appeals or projects concerning some current issue, with television often providing the initial stimulus and information. For example, an item in 'The Clothes Show' about testing products on animals prompted students in an 11–14 school to gather information, design posters, set up a display, organize a petition and approach Blue Peter for support.

Students in a number of schools became involved in the preparations for the United Nations Convention on Children's Rights in the autumn of 1989. Leicestershire is unique in having a Children's Rights Officer, who gave much help and encouragement to one particular group of students in their campaign for greater rights, including the vote at age 14. Following a module on equal opportunities which prompted meetings, petitions, displays and fund raising in school, a girl in year 9 was invited to share a platform (with attendant radio and press coverage) with the Lord Mayor and local MPs. Her commitment to the issues and the increase in her knowledge, as well as her self-esteem, were strongly evident.

Some schools see the development of democratic schooling as a means by which political education is advanced, and are encouraging the extension of student involvement beyond school to work with parish councils and police liaison committees.

Environmental issues are generally of great concern to young people. The lunchtime sound of aluminium cans being crushed for recycling was a feature of some of our visits. In one school a very active recycling group has developed out of a GCSE Humanities assignment on conservation. Students commented that, being better informed as a result of their work, they could articulate their ideas more clearly, argue their case and be more effective in gaining a response. They were concerned to establish an organization which would survive their departure from the school.

Examples have already been cited to illustrate how experiences within the curriculum serve as a catalyst for student-initiated activity outside the curriculum – for teachers, gratifying evidence that they have touched their pupils. An important ingredient in this process is having a climate in which pupils know they can take the initiative and are likely to receive support and encouragement for their ideas – a case of ethos facilitating the release of energy. Sometimes the stimulus comes from outside but the school provides the opportunity and supporting framework for action.

Many of these projects involve fund-raising – pursued with vigour in all the schools for a wide range of beneficiaries. It is important in educational terms to distinguish between simple collections of money, and work which has a planned range of experiences such as awareness raising, research, organization, negotiation, decision-making, committee work, leadership, publicity and keeping accounts.

Many examples could be quoted but the following give some idea of the scope of activities:

- a public concert of dance, music and sketches in aid of the Red Cross Romanian appeal, wholly organized (including advertising, tickets and refreshments) by a group of Year 11 students for whom television news provided the spur
- a sponsored football tournament to raise funds for Ethiopia, which required a range of negotiations and adjustments to plans as the operation proceeded
- an evening of Asian music organized single-handedly by a 13-year-old girl, which attracted 150 people and raised £200 for Children in Need
- the adoption of particular individuals in need – a fellow pupil suffering from leukaemia, a local blind girl, a child in Bangladesh, a premature baby – as the focus for both fund raising and the acquisition of knowledge and understanding

- producing cakes and confectionary for sale (after market research) to provide finance to organize a party for senior citizens
- assisting in the marketing of palm crosses to help a village in Southern Africa
- a programme to involve each year-group in planning a charities week for the benefit of one local, one national and one international charity, with experience of meetings, goal-setting, teamwork and decision-making
- identifying two or three major events (e.g., the local carnival and the school fete) to which fund raising efforts would be directed, as a means of developing parental and community involvement and enhancing the cohesiveness of the school community.

The blurring of the distinction between curricular and extra-curricular activities is furthered by the use of PSE or tutorial time to develop projects which are designed to extend beyond the timetable. Sometimes it may work the other way with pupils negotiating use of curricular time to develop activities begun out of class.

Other pursuits such as the Duke of Edinburgh Award Scheme (which is required to be extra-curricular but is often based in schools, with the help of external support) or membership of outside organizations such as the Red Cross, St John's Ambulance, Guides and Scouts, provide valuable experiences in education for citizenship. In addition, many young people are acting on their own, with groups of friends, or in the context of their own families, in positions of responsibility which provide support for others.

Recognition

The range of considerations outlined so far – in ethos, organizational factors and new styles of teaching and learning – point to the need for fresh approaches to assessment and recognition. The traditional approach with its 'pass/fail' implication, is clearly inappropriate in the field of education for citizenship. Yet great opportunities are missed if the skills, experience and learning associated with the multifarious activities in which pupils are engaged are not made explicit to all concerned. Above all, they must be articulated to, and by, the pupils themselves.

In this context the role of profiles and records of achievement in recognizing the total experience of young people and linking school and community is a development of great potential, not least for the process by which achievements are identified. Schools have worked hard to produce their own styles of documentation, supported by appropriate resources of time and staffing, and it is to be hoped that they receive the recognition outside school that they deserve. Examples we saw range from a single sheet for year 7 summarizing Personal Qualities, Relationships, School Work, Interest and Hobbies, and Aims for Improvement, to detailed task-specific analyses for years 10 and 11 with over 50 categories grouped under Information Skills, Personal and Interpersonal Skills, Creative Skills (Designing, Making and Controlling), Decision Skills and Application/Evaluation Skills. These are supplemented by less formalized personal diaries and continuous self-assessment in relation to individual projects or case studies.

A valuable stimulus to such profiles can come from schemes like the City and Guilds/BTEC Foundation Programmes, which embody the principles that schools are striving for in defining and validating pupils' work, while also offering tangible recognition (i.e., a qualific- ation) of that work. Other aspects of education for citizenship can make a contribution, particularly through course work, to a range of GCSE and A-level courses, to CPVE and other forms of external accreditation. These are most likely to flourish where the general ethos of the school is in harmony with the curriculum experiences of the pupils. A number of the characteristics outlined in our earlier section on ethos, such as the engendering of positive attitudes, of good relationships and of a sense of responsibility, help to prepare pupils for realistic and constructive appraisal of their achievements by negotiation between themselves and the teachers and other adults with whom they are working.

However, quite apart from written records or formal qualifications, there is a clear indication from the young people interviewed that involvement in the kind of experiences described brings its own reward. Two who had placements in primary schools were so stimulated by their role that they phoned each other each evening to share the experiences of the day. Pupils and students referred repeatedly to the fact that they were being trusted and recognized as capable of accepting responsibility. They valued being treated as adults, feeling that they could make a contribution and that it was appreciated, and that they could take decisions, that they had overcome initial fears and nervousness, that they received friendship and love and were able to return it.

Thus, while adults may identify these activities as preparation 'for the opportunities, responsibilities and experiences of adult life', to pupils they have a more immediate value. It is this same immediacy which delights and encourages parents and teachers and suggests that it is by meeting present needs that the future is best pepared for.

Reference

NCC (1989) *Curriculum Guidance 3: The Whole Curriculum*. York: National Curriculum Council.

CHAPTER 6

The Dukeries Community College and Complex: A Case Study

Roy Sowden and Lewis Walker

All schools can become community schools to a greater or lesser extent depending on their location, facilities and philosophy. The Dukeries Community College and Complex is much more than a community school – it is a place where interaction between all ages, abilities and disabilities and all sectors of society is a *raison d'être*, an integral part of education. Thjs Geursen (1985), in his review of informal education for OECD noted that, in the Dukeries, this incidental education – ethos, interaction and informal contacts – is as important as what goes on in timetabled classes. Our objective is to provide a base for people to help themselves to become actively participant at home, at work or at play. Obviously, we encourage them, and hope they will encourage each other, to widen their experiences and to grow. Citizenship, then, is more a way of life than a structured pedagogy, although the College does have a curriculum for Personal and Social Education, negotiation of learning through records of achievement and a broad base of community, outdoor and residential experiences to back this up.

The Dukeries Complex consists of a community college which includes education for c.2000 adults, an under-5s centre, a day centre for the elderly, another for the mentally handicapped called Whitewater, a recreation centre, youth centre, residential training centre, public library and fire training school. It is the base for two parish councils and acts as an agency centre for the probation service, trading standards, community volunteers and the registrar of births, marriages and deaths. Recently the electricity board have put in a machine to dispense tokens for domestic meter payments. A large number of local groups use the theatre and concert hall for meetings and public performances. The College has its own brass band which forms the nucleus of a community band where all ages can play on one evening each week. The library offers an information service and deals with all bookings of the premises and visiting groups. We shall say more about these later but it is perhaps helpful to know a little more about our community and how the Dukeries Complex came into being. The 'school' activities can then be set in the context of the federal structure which values all groups of individuals on campus as participant decision-makers.

The historical context and development of community resources

The village of Ollerton is itself a misnomer as any self-respecting resident of the area will speedily tell you and frequently does. Three villages make up the area. Ollerton, the original Alderston of the Domesday Book, Boughton, another old village some two miles away, and New Ollerton the infill occasioned by the expansion of the coal mines in the 1920s and 1930s. Both of the old villages have had a large number of new homes built around them and the three village complex together with the immediately surrounding area referred to in this article as Ollerton, now has the population of a small town of approximately 13,000 people (NCC, 1983).

The Dukeries Community Comprehensive School was built in 1964 and in the early 1980s began to use space arising from falling rolls to become a wider community facility with the help of the Nottingham-shire County Council, in collaboration with Newark and Sherwood District Council and the Department of Education and Science. Officers asked pupils, teachers, parents, community groups and individuals in the Ollerton district what they would do with the spare space and reported back to the councils in a booklet entitled, *A Place for the Family*. Architects accepted the brief from the compendium of ideas expressed in the booklet, which involved several different client groups – education, social services, leisure services, the clerk's department and the district council. A steering group of senior officers supervised the project. This group included Roy Sowden, the head teacher, who was subsequently invited to become the principal of the Dukeries Complex.

A liaison group of teachers was established early on to ensure architects knew what benefits to teaching might be included in the brief. An informal luncheon group comprising social service workers, heads of local schools, community police, community health workers, librarians, youth workers and others was formed, even before the project began. This group still meets once every two months and discusses problems of concern or new initiatives with the aim of securing mutual support. Issues have ranged from housing to drug abuse, from speech therapy provision to local management of schools. An important inter-agency and volunteer counselling service for young people emerged from one of the early discussions.

Parents joined Sixth Form classes at the same time the college became responsible for adult education in the area. An adult tutor was appointed in addition to making one of the assistant principals responsible for all post-16 work. Adult participation rose immediately from 150 (when a distant FE college had control) to 1500, and numbers of part-time students have consistently been above 1800. School students use the word processors, typewriters and other resources provided for adults and vice-versa. A-level and GCSE choices at 16 + are improved for all. The College provides an additional two-hour session immediately following afternoon school in diverse areas of the curriculum, ranging from electronics to sailing and from writing for profit to horticulture classes. These are open to people of all ages in the community.

Under-5s provision began as a crèche in spare rooms in a disused caretaker's house. It initially served classes and groups meeting on the complex but now includes a toy library (borrow a toy, and you must also borrow a book!) and a baby room. Some parents come for mutual support and a warm friendly place to meet. Staff from social services, adult education, the library and from the College work with parents to build their confidence and to provide learning opportunities. Full-time students on appropriate courses can be placed with the under-5s supervisor for practical experience. Informal strategies for education are recognized as being at least as important as formally structured classes in our context.

The library is open four nights a week and on Saturday mornings. Large-print sections help the elderly and new readers. Primary schools and the College run classes on study skills. College students share the library with the elderly, parents from the under-5s, people with mental handicaps and with young unemployed people.

The Youth Centre offers social and outdoor leadership opportunities to those in school, those who have left school and to junior school children. It is also widely used by those with mental handicaps and for functions requiring disco music. The young people bought all their own lights and disco equipment, which they willingly share with others. Canoes, outdoor pursuits equipment and transport are all shared with others on campus. This is cost-effective and reduces storage. The youth leader runs two lunchtime clubs in cooperation with the College so that older students can see that liaison exists between school and Youth Centre. She also works with the school to provide facilities and leadership for the Duke of Edinburgh Award Scheme.

The Day Centre for the Elderly caters for 30 ambulant elderly each day and makes full use of the Complex facilities for sport, recreation and horticulture. They have provided additional heated greenhouses on the College farm. They are a source of useful information (e.g., GCSE History) and also provide practical experience for full-time students aiming for the caring professions. The mix of ages sharing facilities is a very positive thing, helping to break down barriers and prejudice.

Whitewater is a centre for 125 students with mental handicaps who require day care and teaching. They use the College farm, theatre, library, swimming pool, computer/word processor laboratory and adult literacy classes. They are fully integrated with Complex users including school children, again with positive results for all groups. The riding for the disabled provision pays for all the horse management on the farm – without it the college could not keep this activity going. About 70 school students help with Whitewater activities each week on rota.

The Recreation Centre runs swimming for the community, dry play and pitch rental together with squash and sports facilities paid for by the District Council. There is a comfortable bar, fitness gymnasium and possibilities for 600+ in the sports hall when used as an auditorium. The College and the Recreation Centre share the cost of comfortable seating and this gives flexibility of size for spaces used for public performances and special events. There is a community festival centred on the College Recreation Centre each year.

The Agency Base provides office accommodation for dictrict council and social functions at a modest rental. It houses the registrar of births, marriages and deaths, officers for housing welfare rights, the coordinator for CSV, the probation service, careers and Department of Employment officers and the MP's surgery. The Information and

Library assistants, who run this base, process all lettings for the College.

Organization and management

Central management supports all these agencies and there is a vice principal for Campus and Outreach. The Complex also has a senior administration officer who coordinates all finance, money handling and banking. Reprographics and printing is operated as a central service and recharges departments.

Management is based on wide consultation and overlapping teams. The core Central Management Team is common to College and Community Complex and is briefed by an elected College Committee and a campus Officer Group on policy matters. The principal of the College is also principal of the Complex. We work to an agreed set of objectives to try to enhance the quality of life in the community through interaction, responsive management, mutual benefit and open access to all.

The College governing body operates alongside a Council of Management for the campus. There is cross-linking with the Chair of Governors sitting on the Council of Management and the Vice Chair of Council of Management is a coopted governor. There is a separate Community Budget operated by the principal and answerable to the Council of Management. The delegated school budget (ASB) is supplemented by a non-schools activity budget which pays for the community use of the premises and extra community teaching sessions. There is also a budget for adult education classes to pay for lecturers, materials and some administration. A large number of working parties, committees and task groups help to organize activities, allocate resources and determine policy and these involve all the groups represented on campus.

The College recruits from a family of primary schools in Ollerton and two nearby villages. The teachers are working cooperatively in music and drama where link teachers are appointed and in all the subjects of the National Curriculum, where there is joint training. There are now less than 800 students on roll in a school designed originally for twice that number. There is an active student council which at present is pressing 'green' issues. They successfully campaigned for uniform college dress and engaged the support of parents for their arguments.

Having set the context of where and how our students work, we should now examine some specific strands of their education for citizenship.

Personal and Social Education in the College

A recent review has taken place in order to rationalize the provision for Personal and Social Education in the College. Each student now receives two 1-hour sessions each week, one with their tutor and the other with a more specialist team member. The specialist team cover aspects of health and safety, sex education, political education, the world of work, information technology, and prejudice, discrimination and stereotyping. This involves developing such skills as communication, use of careers information, decision-making, management of stress, group problem-solving and basic parenting skills. It is anticipated that such attitudes as developing a positive self-concept, assertiveness, tolerance, empathy, accepting responsibilities and positive attitudes towards family life will be acquired. Essentially the specialist team utilizes a wide variety of teaching and learning styles in order to achieve their aims and objectives: didactic; group work; active investigational work; individual projects such as work experience. Compulsory Religious Education is also provided in this lesson in years 10 and 11.

The second session is seen as complementary and interactive with the specialist provision. The tutors are supported by an extended team taken from the entire staff to allow a flexible programme of active tutorial work, counselling and review to take place. This encompasses the processes central to producing records of achievement.

The first years' programme (year 7) for instance, includes an induction to the Complex during the first term, relating to others during the second term and an emphasis on study skills and self-assessment during the final term. Any insularity that may exist in some schools is broken down here by planned visits to every area of the Complex. Students begin to appreciate the two-way process of the mutual benefit joined from extraordinarily good resources and the contribution they can make to our community.

Two further fundamental aspects of the programme are role play and having visitors in classrooms. Role play helps to break down the barriers and create different relationships between tutor and tutor group to that of classroom teacher and class group. Again, different styles of teaching are required: discussing topics, small group work, lots of movement and talk. In-service training has been required and provided for staff and there is now excellent support for this work. Visitors are invited from within and outside the Complex. Students learn to plan, organize and host visits. The skills acquired are seen as very important in the world of work and indeed throughout life.

Outdoor Pursuits

Outdoor Pursuits has long been an established part of the Dukeries curriculum. The head of Outdoor Pursuits works a flexi-timetable in order to accommodate community groups and provide weekend trips and camps. We endeavour to provide every child at the Dukeries with a residential experience as part of their entitlement curriculum and Outdoor Pursuits plays a vital role in this. In recent years we have extended the base provision of 6 weekend treks and a 2-week camp in the Lake District and focused on year 8 by also using the LEA's Field Study centres in the Peak District for Outdoor Pursuits, Environmental Education, Science and Geography fieldwork. Timetabled camp craft in year 10 establishes a firm foundation for further activities as does a variety of Session 11 activities such as sailing, navigation studies, windsurfing and canoeing. 'It's like PSE time being extended over days – it's an opportunity to follow things through with a captive audience', said the head of Outdoor Pursuits. On camp the aims are to allow students to accept responsibility, to work in teams and to live harmoniously together. The students have an opportunity to utilize all the skills covered in school. The residential experience allows for practical application, taking control, and response to a challenging situation. It is no wonder that the majority of those who attend camp return again and many ex-students also wish to participate. The camp is first set up beforehand by asking students which group they wish to work with. They then have to function as a working unit and problems are sorted out within the group. By the end of each week students are working in an effective unit, well-organized and relating well to the whole camp. The groups often plan their own routes and within a controlled situation are expected to solve and rectify any errors. The teachers feel this is a major place to learn and for most of the time are merely guiding choice and judgement.

For a long time the College has produced a certificate of achievement for the activities completed. Recently, however, we have joined a county-wide initiative called the Nottinghamshire Trailblazer Scheme. It will be an extension to our existing work which gives credit and recognition to achievement in Environmental Education and Outdoor

Pursuits. It seeks to strengthen each pupil's skills and competencies in adventure and challenge, environmental knowledge, understanding and concern, PSE and community service through conservation and rescue.

Fieldwork is so fundamental to Geography that it has been made an essential part of every student's course, from year 10 students studying their 'home area', to consortium arrangements for post-16 students which takes them to Aberystwyth for a week each year. We have always stressed the importance of fieldwork and our students enjoy the experience of making their studies realistic.

Needless to say students who have difficulties over finance are supported from both official and voluntary funds.

Record of achievement and work experience

Before the College joined The East Midlands Record of Achievement Pilot in 1985, a paper presented by a staff working party on pupil profiles strongly recommended a scheme which would be developmental and aimed at promoting self-awareness. It incorporated target-setting, individualized and possibly contracted learning and joint pupil–teacher assessment and recording. Since then it has become clear that there is considerable benefit to the pupils from the variety of processes being used to create records of achievement. Target-setting and review related to mainstream curriculum objectives are fundamental to the long-term success of records of achievement. It is also hoped that, in time, similar assessment procedures will apply to the National Curriculum. In 1989 a full Record of Personal Achievement was issued to all Dukeries year 11 students.

Work leading towards a record of achievement is totally integrated into the PSE and tutorial work of the College. The close relationship between the two areas of work is forged because the PSE specialist team have assisted year coordinators, providing a complete package of materials; tutors are therefore able to follow guidelines provided for them. Heads of year ensure that these guidelines are followed and that deadlines are met. Tutors have three sources of support, therefore, through their heads of year, through the specialist PSE team and through additional staff not directly allocated a tutor group.

Assessment is an acknowledged part of the education process and when based upon criterion referencing and student personal referencing its purposes are ones which improve motivation, provide a base for future targeting, as well as informing others such as parents, tutors, potential employers and other institutions. The involvement of the students themselves in the process and the subsequent negotiation of learning are seen as the key issues in assessment. Assessment and reporting may be divided into two separate but inter-related areas: the formative process and the summative process.

Each department at the Dukeries has its own style of formative recording. However, classroom practice and the design of the documentation is based on the principles of target-setting, criteria referencing, feedback and outcomes. Feedback as a basis for remedial action and further motivation is available to all students. In this way the formative record encourages and demonstrates progression by recognizing positive achievement and identifying weaknesses related to evidence and context.

The College takes a wide view of the experiences and achievements which can contribute to a record of achievement: none more important than work experience which is available for two weeks to all students in year 10 and all post-16 students. In the spring term of year 10, all students write a letter of application for a work experience place, selecting a first, second and third choice. They fill in a preparation booklet in which they are able to set personal goals. They are given considerable information about placements and the purposes and procedures of work experience. All students fill in a work experience diary while on their placement and upon their return to College they complete a summary sheet in a PSE class. The summary is obtained through a structured note-making process using the work experience diary, the specialist PSE staff and sometimes the tutors involved in visiting students during their placement. The preparation activities are believed to be useful in giving students confidence in the work place, while the diary gives them detailed evidence for the construction of the summative work experience statement.

We are now building work experience into the wider curriculum, especially at post-16. As well as work-shadowing exercises and devising modules of work based on students' work experience, further work is being done to explore job roles at management level. There is a 15-day minimum work experience placement for students on the highly successful CPVE course. There is preparation, review and a policy of relating placements to vocational modules. Placements are subject to further fine-tuning as vocational modules become more specialized.

Negotiated learning

If knowledge, skills, attitudes and concepts are something to be transmitted to a child, then a view of citizenship is already implied insofar as what matters is obedience, passivity and non-questioning students. If, however, we take the model which describes a citizen in terms of an active, informed, critical participant in a democracy then we are also sending out a set of important signals to our students. The Dukeries has taken on board this model of active participation and this has an instant implication for the way we teach and conduct ourselves in classrooms and for the powerful area of learning we often call the 'hidden' curriculum.

We believe that classrooms should be places where students' views are respected, valued and given some recognition. The main vehicle has been the record of achievement processes but the philosophy has to be integral to the whole curriculum. The Dukeries Complex with its many and varied employees and resources is crucial in this interaction. Our job is about moving horizons and activating the imagination. Schools, alone, can inhibit development in citizenship because they are closed, too secure from external influence, or just by the very nature of the way a school day is arranged.

We are trying hard not to 'tell' our students all the time but to empower them along with other members of our community. We might have the best intentions in the world but the way in which we tackle the subject predetermines the outcome. For instance, there is a sense in which empowerment is accessible to all ages and abilities: just the questioning attitude as opposed to passive obedience is one which can be encouraged.

College Council is a good example of this. Democracy is practised progressively through from tutor group representation to year councils and finally the College Council. College Council is a real attempt to empower students: to air their views; to bring new ideas to the forefront and to modify old ones; air grievances; provide alternative strategies for problem-solving. Perhaps the most important factor of all is making students feel that they have a significant role to play in the running of the college.

Cross-curricular citizenship

The focus on citizenship at the Dukeries is across the curriculum. Aspects are easily recognized in post-16 education through courses such as Law in Society, Psychology, Sociology and CPVE core studies. Problem-solving and social skills are developed through CPVE integrated projects, not by individual subjects. Students have to show involvement in issues at the same time as academic work. During

CPVE community-based projects, involvement is recognized and recorded and the 'running a small business' project brings out the nature of ethics in the business world.

Community service for years 10 and 11 also allows students the opportunity to contribute and to find a different niche for themselves. Failure to achieve in one area can so easily transfer to another in the same environment. The opportunity to succeed in a community sphere is invariably taken. Children must be given chances to succeed and feel worthy if they are to have the confidence in themselves and to contribute to society.

The concept of bias features overtly in the year 10 and 11 curriculum when the English department examines persuasive writing. This is a syllabus obligation and not conceived on a citizenship model. However, the work makes a contribution through its critical strand. Students are asked to make a series of decisions based on an understanding of the quality of information received.

There are two schemes of work for the units of critical understanding of information. One looks at the invention of marketing of a national product, the other follows the same process but with a rock group or whoever. The work seeks to explore how people set out to persuade and then turns it on its head and encourages students to employ persuasive language on their own account. It gives students the capacity to recognize bias, to recognize that no language is innocent and that there is no way of saying something that is not influenced by your own ideological position.

The input from Drama is another example of the cross-curricular citizenship theme. The first theme in year 7 for Drama is 'communities'. Work is developed in an imaginative way to build a particular community. The aim is to start groups working together, confront problems together and solve problems together. The emphasis is on the group to begin with, followed by an examination of the actions of individuals. The work encourages the kind of virtues which are encompassed in the documents about citizenship. When asked why we still continue to fail on some occasions, the head of Drama replied:

> Without imagination it's very difficult to put yourself in the place of others and it's also very difficult then to take any responsibility for your own behaviour. Because if you haven't put yourself in the place of somebody who has been disturbed by your behaviour in whatever way it is, if you only see things through your own eyes, if you can't act or think as 'if' it were somebody else, you can't take on the emotion. Then

you have a very blinkered version of life and you have no way of realising your behaviour influences anybody else or even caring it does.

Conclusion

There is a great danger that, in a lot of important senses, schools may be redesigned to eliminate all the complex variables that everyday citizenship is about. In many ways life in school can be artificial in terms of what happens outside school. What happens outside should not be experienced by students as a bonus but should take place as often as possible.

Citizenship should grow out of everyday life with an institutional awareness that it is part and parcel of everyday teaching. We cannot actually timetable 'caring' but we can provide opportunities which arise out of individual, group, teacher or student needs. The work done in structured curriculum time, particularly PSE, encourages some aspects of good citizenship, but a subject identified as citizenship would perhaps exclude some of the most important features such as mutuality, cooperation with others, shared responsibility, and learning how to manage common goals and purposes.

The five guiding principles of the Dukeries Complex allow us a chance to follow a common course and to live our lives as good citizens. We try to widen horizons, to help to improve the quality of life in the area by offering support and guidance towards learning, participation and self-development, and by providing entertainment and fun. There is an expectation of mutual cooperation and therefore mutual benefit. The holistic management principle is one which removes boundaries and allows people with different experience and professionalism to improve our own practices. We are here to give access to all facilities and to build the confidence of all our clients, both real and potential. By actively seeking ways of getting groups working together and sharing resources we can do much to help our community beyond the boundaries of the Dukeries Complex.

References

Guersen, T. (1985) *Facilities for Formal and Informal Education*. Paris: UNESCO.

NCC (1983) *A Place for the Family*. Mimeo. Nottingham: Nottinghamshire County Council.

CHAPTER 7

Citizenship in Schools

George Gyte and Danielle Hill

The task of education in the next decade will be to prepare youngsters to fulfil a rewarding and participative role in a complex democratic society. The world which awaits them has high expectations. Tomorrow's citizens will need a range of transferable skills to respond creatively to tomorrow's fast changing scene.

In order to prepare the children to meet these demands, young people are entitled to access to a wide range of experiences which will stretch their knowledge and understanding in a multitude of ways. Preparation for the world of adult life should make them aware not only of their rights but also of the responsibilities which underpin these rights.

Responsibilities and rights are not learned in a discrete slot once a week but stem from a range of learning experiences. Classrooms which empower pupils to take responsibility for their learning and work collaboratively play a key role in this apprenticeship. These processes will only occur in institutions where concepts of fairness and justice are pivotal to the ethos. This climate will give a high priority to equality of opportunity and will help all concerned to value and celebrate the pluralism of our global community. This is the real educational challenge of the 1990s. It is within this context that we must perceive education for citizenship.

The present context for citizenship in schools

Schools are concerned about the concept of citizenship and how they should best meet the challenges it offers. This was illustrated by the response given to the National Survey carried out by Leicester University on behalf of the Commission on Citizenship. Eight hundred questionnaires were circulated and 455 were returned.

As Fogelman (1990) points out: 'given the extremely tight timetable and the other many demands on schools, this is a very satisfactory response, in itself indicating the high level of interest and enthusiasm for this topic in many schools'.

This response reflects the statutory responsibility placed upon schools by the Education Reform Act 1988 (ERA) to provide a broad, balanced curriculum which: 'promotes the spiritual, moral, cultural, mental and physical development at the school and of society' and 'prepares pupils for the opportunities, responsibilities and experiences of adult life'.

The Whole Curriculum (NCC, 1990a) has highlighted the need for schools to address the above requirements through a variety of curricular and extra curricular experiences. Elements have been identified which, in the context of Personal and Social Education, will ensure coherence across the whole curriculum. The principal elements which will enable schools to address these requirements have been identified as dimensions, skills and cross-curricular themes. The dimensions have been acknowledged as permeating across the curriculum, hence they influence the ethos of the school and consequently embody the whole issue of equal opportunities. Race, gender and ability have been identified as the three strands of equal opportunities. The skills which should provide a common bond to the curriculum are those of communication, numeracy, study, problem-solving, and Information Technology and are relevant to personal and social growth and education. The five themes identified by the National Curriculum Council (1990a) are: Economic and Industrial Understanding, Careers Education and Guidance, Health Education, Environmental Education and Citizenship. It is assumed at this stage that 'they are essential parts of the whole curriculum'.

At the point of writing, NCC Guidance 8 for Education on Citizenship has not been published. However a useful summary appears in *Curriculum Guidance 3* (NCC, 1990a) and the Commission on Citizenship has also produced its report *Encouraging Citizenship* (HMSO, 1990). These two documents provide a challenging context for the debate.

Citizenship and, consequently, preparation to fulfil one's role in society, does not come to a halt at 16+. *Core Skills 16-19* (NCC,

1990f) stresses the need for skills, dimensions and themes to be developed within the context of the 16–19 situation. Though it was expected that the emphasis on skills, in keeping with the report *Towards a Skills Revolution* (CBI, 1989) would be given a high profile, the five themes are also seen as 'essential in the post-16 curriculum'.

The National Curriculum Council (1990a) has identified the aims of education for Citizenship as to 'establish the importance of positive, participative citizenship and provide the motivation to join' and also 'help pupils to acquire and understand essential information on which to base the development of their skills, values and attitudes towards citizenship'.

Educating for democracy has for some time been high on certain agendas. Many could have identified with the rationale provided by Colin Wringe (1984), who perceived educating for democracy as implying helping future citizens 'to understand society and to live and operate effectively within it'.

The many initiatives which have affected schools and colleges over the last ten years, have enabled most of the educational world to accept that our educational institutions do not stand alone. They endeavour to reflect and meet the needs of the many constituencies they serve. The Green Paper (DES, 1977) reported the mismatches between the baggage youngsters have acquired in schools and the expectations of employers, and hinted at the responsibility of educational institutions to redress the balance. Thirteen years later, preparation for the world of work, and industry links as defined by the Schools Council Industry Project (SCIP) through industry, by industry, have been welcomed as a means of enriching the curriculum diet of all students. Excellent opportunities have been created across the phases to tap into this resource. Primary schools have shown how they can take a lead in this domain which at first had been identified as the prerogative of secondary education.

One of the components which is likely to form the backbone of the National Curriculum Council final guidance document is the need to prepare youngsters to function as individuals in a variety of groups, from the most immediate and familiar such as their family, the school, the community and extending to the country they live in and beyond. It will also stress the need to be aware of a variety of other groups which are meaningful (or should be) to individuals in adult life; from national bodies such as the government, to European and global organizations. Opening this franchise matters since, as Pike and Selby (1986) remind us: 'almost all of us are caught up in a network of links, interaction and relationships that circle the planet like a giant and intricate spider's web'. The main issues of our time such as un-employment, environmental pollution, etc., make it very difficult to offer a useful and productive explanation on a purely local or even national level.

Though the idea of education for citizenship has at times been somewhat nebulous, it is not new. In the 1930s the Association for Education in Citizenship aimed 'to advance the study of training and citizenship by which is meant training to the moral equalities necessary for citizens of a democracy, the encouraging of clear thinking about everyday affairs' (Centre for Contemporary Cultural Studies, 1981). The National Curriculum Council stresses that strategies available to students to address the themes must reflect the fact that they are to be cemented through knowledge, understanding, skills and attitudes. The Commission on Citizenship's (1990) report highlights that young people should leave school equipped with the tools which will enable them to participate fully in society. The skills which will free youngsters to lead a productive life in our democratic society and ensure that they can resolve conflict and project their case effectively are identified as the capacity to debate, argue and present a coherent point of view; participating in elections; taking responsibility by repre-senting others, for example on a school council; working collabor-atively; playing as a member of a team; protesting, for example, by writing to a newspaper or councillor, or a local store.

In acquiring and developing the above skills, which will involve knowledge, understanding and attitudes to be developed within a given context, the issue of affective development versus acquisition of knowledge needs to be addressed. Personal and Social Education is traditionally a recognized domain where emotions and feelings can be acknowledged. Health Education particularly has forced us to recognize that 'Emotion involves cognition and conversely our cognitions are permeated by emotions and by our values' (White, 1989).

The themes, though not devoid of context, are still heavily process based, and offer the means to ensure that a wide range of learning styles and teaching approaches are used across the curriculum. The variety of these has been well rehearsed (pair work, group work, etc.). They all contribute to extending the role of the teacher to one of a manager of the learning environment. *Curriculum Guidance 3* (NCC, 1990a) declares boldly that 'the wide range of skills pupils must acquire must be reflected in an equally wide variety of approaches to teaching'. Here is the key to empowering pupils to take an active part in their learning.

Preparation for life in a plural society has been featured as a prerequisite of education for citizenship. The Swann Report (HMSO, 1985a), made a strong commitment to education for all, stressing that multicultural education is not necessarily about providing cultural experiences for young people from ethnic minorities, but is above all about enabling all pupils to understand the nature of our pluralist society. Though the report hinted that we should not only recognize this diversity but celebrate it, it has been said that it fell short of making a strong commitment to tackling issues of racism. Equality of opportunities, as defined by the National Curriculum Council, encompasses not only issues of assessing the curriculum but of outcomes; this is to be welcomed. It should foster a climate within our educational institutions which enables them to go beyond a commonly accepted role of PSE, which is 'to ensure that children acquire knowledge, values and attitudes appropriate to critical and racial diversity' (White, 1989), and permeate these issues, beliefs and attitudes across the whole institution.

The NCC (1990a) also urges schools to take account of gender issues and recognizes that certain attitudes need to be challenged if performance in some curricular areas is to be improved. The issue of ability and accessing the curriculum was addressed in *Curriculum Guidance 2*, (NCC, 1989) which by concentrating on the matter of assessing the curriculum, focuses on matters of differentiation.

It was acknowledged earlier on that schools have a multiplicity of views on what the study of education for citizenship entails. This in itself might be seen as a creative forum, ripe for further challenging and stimulating developments; however the time has come to seek out the perspectives of young people in this issue.

How do they see their curricular experiences preparing them for the world of adult life? Do they feel adequately equipped to participate in a democratic society? Pike and Selby (1986) suggest that 'schools fail in two of their most basic functions: to enable students to make sense of the world in which they live and to endow them with the skills and insights necessary for effective participation in a democratic society'. They identify the main role assigned to schools in the field of Personal and Social development as twofold: one aspect of the task relates to enabling/empowering young people to make the 'journey outwards'. This could be translated in terms of preparing our students for life after school, with all that this entails. The other aspect is identified as the 'journey inwards', meaning that educational establishments do not always succeed in helping students to assess their capabilities and understand their positions regarding the values and attitudes they carry with them and how they reflect on their interaction with their immediate community and wider nation-wide or global issues.

The Prince's Trust commissioned the Social and Community Planning Research organization to carry out a survey to seek out the views of young people on citizenship and volunteering. The survey (SCPR, 1989) revealed that all interviewed would have welcomed the opportunity to learn about citizenship while still at school. Several comments are disturbing and should work as a stimulus to make us review our practice. One 17-year-old expressed his regret this way: 'You should know about it. It's your life, it's your community – and you really have a responsibility to yourself to know about it ... it should be taught'. A university student's comment referred to a host of issues also embedded in the teaching of citizenship:

> 'What you're taught at school is to obey what you are told to do by a teacher. That is absolutely opposed to good citizenship. Good citizenship is that you use your brain and teach yourself about things. What you're told to do is: 'don't question, just do what you're told'. You're actually being taught to be a bad unresponsive, passive, stupid citizen'.

This seems an appropriate moment to start focusing on how one can help maximize the opportunities available within the context of educating for citizenship. We would like to approach this following section in two parts. First, we shall explore what citizenship means, as a discrete component, then endeavour to define the Northamptonshire view of citizenship within the context of cross-curricularity.

The rationale for education for citizenship

Citizenship as a whole curriculum

Within our present educational climate, it is essential to stress that schools and colleges suffer from a severe case of overload. Consequently, one of the prerequisites for any strategy will be to suggest strategies which are manageable.

Any developments in this field will need to address the nature of organizations which can either facilitate or hinder, through certain approaches and developments, the processes of learning. This will centre around the following questions: how are pupils encouraged to take responsibility for their learning? How are opportunities created for pupils to achieve? How does the school enable pupils to value their own and other's work and to discuss it in a positive, supportive manner? Do pupils have the opportunity to work in a variety of different group sizes? What criteria are used to manage these groups? It is possible for pupils to exercise imagination and insight and express these through a variety of media, including group work, role play and drama? Finally, are there opportunities created for reflecting on experiences, is there enough time made available to help affective growth against the security of a sound cognitive input?

Research on moral education shows that there is progression in moral reasoning as there is progression in acquisition of cognitive skills. It is crucial in this area of work not to underplay the acquisition of skills and concepts which enable young people to grow in moral stature; even if we accept that acting morally requires operating according to agreed principles, thinking through the consequences of what one is about to do requires cognitive ability.

Equal opportunities must also underpin any thinking in the area of education for citizenship. It has implications for accessing the curriculum and monitoring outcomes in our institutions, and for preparation for life in a multicultural, multi-racial community. Recognizing achievement in this area of work must be given a high profile and cover the multi-faceted initiatives youngsters may become involved with.

A constructive debate can only be triggered off in a climate where attention has been given to pupils' groupings, staff deployment and resource allocation. Care should be taken for young people to experience relationships within a range of contexts in order to develop social skills, understanding and personal qualities which will enable them to function effectively in adult life.

That the community is a central resource to educating for citizenship must be stipulated. This will manifest itself under many guises; involving the community within the school and more precisely the classroom and will also offer opportunities for the outward looking curriculum, and provide challenging experiences beyond the classroom.

Encouraging Citizenship (Commission on Citizenship, 1990) is committed to an approach which will offer an opportunity to know and understand how our democratic society works, and to experiences of learning through the community: 'We believe that the development of skills and experience of community are equally vital components of such an educational experience'. This position requires that young people leave school with the appropriate skills to participate actively in the society in which they live.

This has been recognized by Wringe (1984): 'Certain skills and attributes may be a necessary condition for participating in government, as they are in any other distinct activity'. How are schools to facilitate the acquisition of key processes to achieve this aim? Much has been written about the role of the ethos in any establishment. Some writers have referred to the 'hidden curriculum', implying that what matters is not what is acquired through the formal, accepted positional statement of an institution, but the unwritten codes of practice, which are recognized by all (pupils, teachers and non-teaching staff) as the unwritten rules which have to be adhered to. How do schools create an atmosphere which will best encourage youngsters to perceive that not only have they an entitlement, but also a responsibility to take an active part in our democratic institutions? This growth can only occur in an establishment which values its students, offers an opportunity through learning situations to learn collaboratively, to develop analytical skills which will empower them to make decisions after the consideration of factual information, to work as a team and be encouraged to take risks within a safe learning environment. This regime will enable pupils to understand the world around them, to ascertain how they function within various groupings, and will help them to examine structures which can directly offer pupils experiences of democratic activities.

Ungoed Thomas (1972) pointed out the varied ways democratic activity may be encouraged at school level. He advocated the use of school councils as a useful strategy. One objection directed to the development feared that school councils would only provide education in participant democracy for the many, and education in leadership for the few. This concern reinforces the need for school councils to evolve in an atmosphere which will allow involvement and decision-making to occur at various levels.

The starting point should be the classroom which allows learners to take responsibility for their learning. Young people should be exposed to experiences which should facilitate their mastering concepts under-lining the democratic process, such as the need to understand that one's personal viewpoint will not necessarily win the day. Operating successfully within the democratic mode requires many opportunities to practice appropriate skills. However, though all agree that young people whose literacy and numeracy skills are deemed defective require further coaching and practice, this has not applied so far to the acquisition of democratic skills.

This issue has implications for a whole range of potential involvements with which we would wish our students to become involved. The Commission on Citizenship (1990) took as its main thrust the notion of active citizenship, which has its roots in community involvement: 'we believe that belonging to a community, which is a core element of citizenship, needs to be fostered; and that ideally all young people should feel that they belong and have a contribution of value to make, if they so wish'. Preparation and support for such activities must also be provided after the statutory leaving age: 'if adequate support is to be made available to enable men and women to organise themselves, and influence decision making totally and nationally, Adult Education and community development are of paramount importance'.

The need to develop social, planning, organizational, negotiating and debating skills is perceived as pivotal to the theme of citizenship. This could be seen as relating to the skills introduced through many Personal and Social Education courses which aim to foster such things as self-assessment, making choices and taking initiatives. This was acknowleded by White (1973) who recommended that '(a person) knows about as many initiatives or ways of life as possible which he [sic] may want to choose for their own sake' and 'that he is able to reflect on priorities among them from the point of view not only of the present moment but as far as possible his life as a whole'. Hence the rationale for education for citizenship is to establish the importance of positive and participative approaches to citizenship. This can only be achieved by helping pupils acquire and understand essential information on which to base the development of their skills, values and attitudes towards citizenship. This field of experience and knowledge should also provide the opportunity to redress the balance between emphasis on the individual and its relationship to a group (or groups). It has been said that over the last twenty years prominence has been given to the individual. Needless to say, within an educational context, it is fitting to seek to address individual educational needs. However, in a wider context, stressing the condition of the self-reliant individual competing against others can lead to the fragmentation of a cohesive society. There is a great deal to be gained by empowering individuals to become involved in strong and targeted task groups, which will enable them to affect their immediate environment.

Citizenship: theme or dimension?

Readjusting the balance between the individual and the group naturally leads to the matter of rights and responsibilities. It is undeniable that citizens have rights; however, rights are underpinned by responsibilities. It is important for the young people in our educational establishments to be made aware of this close relationship. This complex notion was very much on the agenda when Northamptonshire Local Education Authority and Northamptonshire Police reviewed their working practices in schools. The rationale for the partnership was couched in terms of fairness and justice, and the interaction between the rights and responsibilities of individuals. Both departments perceived that developments in this area could lock into citizenship initiatives. That is why we decided that our police school liaison input would be threaded across the curriculum, and rely on joint planning involving both teacher and police officer. The joint secondment of a police officer and teacher produced a document 'Good PALS' which, through its mapping exercises, suggested how areas of work relating to citizenship could be threaded across the curriculum throughout the four key stages. It is intended that this strategy of enriching the curriculum will contribute towards developing young people who are personally autonomous, but capable of good relationships with others and adept at working in groups for the common good.

I stressed earlier that in order to motivate institutions to take on board the concept of citizenship it will be necessary to present it as an issue which can be managed successfully within the whole curriculum. Non-statutory guidance is already available on the other four themes: industrial and economic understanding, health education, careers education and guidance, and environmental education.

It is helpful at this stage to seek elements of commonality between the themes. All five themes have been defined as an entitlement that all learners must access. They all require attention to be given to knowledge, understanding, skills and attitudes. Their basic agenda, preparation for the world of adult life, creates the opportunity for schools to address the five themes within the context of cross-curricularity. The underpinning principles for such an approach are inherent within the themes themselves, since they seek to enable young people to acquire knowledge, competencies and qualifications for a highly complex technological society. En route, they provide opportunities for learners to solve problems, work in teams, be enterprising, creative, function as effective individuals, and consequently empower pupils to take an active part in the learning process.

Cross-curricularity rests on the interaction between the themes and the dimensions. All five themes demand a high commitment to equality of opportunities. For instance, economic and industrial understanding stresses the need to explore and combat stereotypes: 'schools should be aware of pupils' attitudes and assumptions which relate to this component of the curriculum, for example, gender stereotypes about technology as a subject and engineering as a career' (NCC, 1990b). The same document celebrates an opportunity to allow youngsters with special learning needs to be able to achieve via different routes: 'some pupils will benefit from teaching approaches which make best use of their oral strengths and avoid their difficulties with written communication, for example, through appropriate use of tape recorders'.

All themes recommend that schools should consider ways of recording pupils' experiences, so as to acknowledge the contribution of cross-curricular themes to their personal development, hence widening the franchise for recording achievement. The careers education and guidance document (NCC, 1990d) stresses the connection between records of achievement and action plans.

All five themes also deal with controversial issues such as the impact of economic activity on the environment, sex education (including AIDS education and the misuse of drugs). These concerns can be difficult to approach since, 'telling people about the environment can provoke a response of alarm and rejection rather than encouraging them to find out more and take action' (NCC, 1990e).

All themes require a rationale expressed through school policies to ensure that issues of continuity and progression are addressed, and to avoid unnecessary repetition while encouraging, within the context of the spiral curriculum, certain topics to be revisited and expanded to meet the needs of learners throughout the four key stages and beyond. They also encourage the use of adults other than teachers across the curriculum, and firmly perceive the community as a resource. They act as a pivotal trigger for the outward looking curriculum: work experience, community experience and visits to such places as industrial complexes, nature parks, and magistrates courts can all contribute to an enriched curriculum.

All themes can lock into existing attainment targets when appropriate. All guidance documents state emphatically that all themes are inter-related, since 'they share many features, for example, the capacity to promote discussion of value and belief, and to extend knowledge, skills and understanding' (NCC, 1990c).

A brief summary of the outlining rationale for the four themes additional to citizenship will prove helpful.

Careers education sets out to prepare pupils for the responsibilities of adult life and help them understand the role they will have in life by equipping them to make choices, responding positively to changes and transitions, and knowing themselves better. In order to meet these targets they will require direct experiences of work and links with the community outside the school. *Education for economic and industrial understanding* addresses issues relating to rights of consumers, needs of producers, and throughout the key stages moves from local topics to regional, European and global concerns. In so doing, it prepares young people for their future economic role as producers, consumers and citizens in a democracy. The *raison d'être* of *health education* rests on the following statement: 'people's health is one of the most important products that any society can create and one of the most important resources required for the creation of any kind of wealth' (NCC, 1990c). A coherent health education programme will encourage the establishment of healthy patterns of behaviour, enable people to make appropriate choices about life styles and contribute to the development of a healthy population. It stresses that the responsibility for health education should be shared with others. It highlights three focuses for study: the individual, the group and the wider community. Finally, *environmental education* aims to: 'provide opportunities to acquire knowledge, values, attitudes, commitment and skills needed to protect and improve the environment, encourage pupils to examine and interpret the environment from a variety of perspectives and arouse pupils' awareness and curiosity to encourage active participation in resolving environmental problems' (NCC, 1990e).

Citizenship: the overarching umbrella

All four themes have a great deal in common with education for citizenship; they all attempt to help young people make sense of the world of adult life; they have shifting focuses which centre on the individual and his/her interactions to a variety of groups. Above all, they all stress the need for active participation. My contention is that all these themes help satisfy some of the aims underpinning the aims of education for citizenship.

How can we ensure that citizenship can provide the matrix which will facilitate the interaction between the themes and dimensions within the context of cross-curricularity? It has been said that the themes, though not devoid of process, are content based. The brief overview from *Curriculum Guidance 3*, (NCC, 1990a) outlining the areas of study for citizenship, satisfies this claim. The content will ensure acquisition of knowledge about electoral procedures, local and national government, to name but a few areas. It will also address issues of social, civil and political entitlements, obligations and responsibilities, as highlighted in the last category in the same section of the guidance document which refers to being a citizen, and stresses the need to explore relationships between rights and privileges and emphasizes the 'importance of participating'.

In order to satisfy this last requirement, schools need to address issues of ethos: what sort of organizational models should be developed? How can all members of the school community be valued? Are there appropriate mechanisms to recognize and record a variety of achievements? How does the school relate to the community? Is the community perceived as a learning resource? Are pupils keen to contribute towards helping their community? Is it established school policy to help pupils realize their relationship and allegiance to various groups, including the global community? And last, what kinds of democratic principles and practices operate in schools; what are the opportunities to acquire democratic skills and take on board real responsibilities?

These processes which in turn will ensure that equal opportunities in the establishment can become a reality, require a whole-school approach and highlight the 'dimension quality' of citizenship. Consequently, citizenship provides the matrix which enables the cross-fertilization of dimensions and themes, and will also provide the appropriate backcloth for Health and Environmental Education to be developed as whole-school approaches which foster the well being and self-esteem of individuals in a respected environment.

Hence citizenship becomes an interesting hybrid: as a dimension it alludes to school ethos, democratic processes and interaction between groups, and becomes an all-pervading whole-school approach, which demands a school management strategy. As a theme, and consequently content-based, it can also provide opportunities for young people to acquire the necessary skills and knowledge to exercise their democratic rights and responsibilities. The overriding component in this matrix will vary across the key stages. Citizenship as a dimension will be more prominent throughout the first two key stages, whereas more attention will be required on the content-based theme at later points. However, it would be unwise to undervalue the importance of the ethos of any institution since it is central to the successful delivery of the curriculum.

This approach to cross-curricular themes and dimensions enables institutions to address this area in a less fragmented way. Much has been said of the need to audit the curriculum and map out appropriate pathways. Our experience is that we can all lose ourselves in the mapping and auditing processes of where we want to go and how we intend to get there. Of course, there is an undeniable case to be made for sound planning; after all, endless repetitions and lack of progression have for too long marred many developments in this field. The recommended approach should enable us to take on new challenges with a minimum of disruption by changing the focus or emphasis of our existing practice. The way of testing out this theory could be the adoption of European Awareness which would enable progression within the world of work to cumulate in European work experience.

Our close examination of the interaction between the themes has above all highlighted what most of us already know, that some of these issues have been with us for some time and, in many instances, addressed in challenging ways. However, having a clear view of the kind of curricular experiences we want our young people to encounter will help us sharpen our practice and decide where we want to address specific developments, be it across the curriculum or as a discrete PSE slot.

Using citizenship as a rationalization to cross-curricularity raises a key question: what of Personal and Social Education? Is citizenship to supersede PSE? Most of the processes associated with PSE can be identified in the proposed model, though colleagues would argue that there are key areas which have not been acknowledged, including a pragmatic one: the role of PSE in the formative process of recording achievement. Is PSE to be used as a coordinating mechanism throughout the school to ensure the delivery of citizenship? An interesting dilemma.

The model developed in this chapter will provide a set of outcomes for evaluation. A few central indicators could be used to test out the nature of the school community links, links with employers, display of children's work, responses to behavioural difficulties and attendance.

Better Schools (DES, 1985b) identified a major objective of education 5–16 as being 'to help pupils acquire understanding, knowledge and skills relevant to adult life and employment in a fast changing world'. The proposed model will provide young people with the skills, knowledge and understanding necessary to assume the role of the active citizen. It is worth placing the emphasis on skills, since as 'much in the future is uncertain; what is beyond dispute is that in the next century these skills, together with flexibility and adaptability, will be at a premium' (NCC, 1990a). It is important for us all to have a vision of what kind of experiences pupils should encounter. This vision has to reflect local, regional, national, European and global intentions. Education for the citizens of tomorrow's world must seek to help them map out te network of interdependencies which sustains us all.

Our strategy should be guided by a strong commitment to enabling our young people to make sense of their learning experiences. It will also acknowledge that pupils do not grow in a school where teachers do not develop professionally, since as the Hadow Report (Board of Education, 1931) pointed out, 'a good school, in short, is not a place of compulsory instruction, but a community of old and young people engaged in learning by cooperative experiment'.

CITIZENSHIP
A MATRIX FOR CROSS-CURRICULARITY

Citizenship as a dimension: Economic and Industrial Understanding; Health Education; Careers Education and Guidance; Environmental Education.

SCHOOL ETHOS

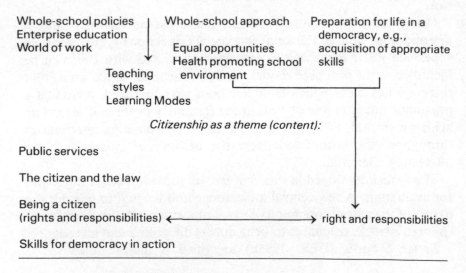

Whole-school policies
Enterprise education
World of work

Whole-school approach

Equal opportunities
Health promoting school
environment

Preparation for life in a
democracy, e.g.,
acquisition of appropriate
skills

Teaching
styles
Learning Modes

Citizenship as a theme (content):

Public services

The citizen and the law

Being a citizen
(rights and responsibilities) ←——————————→ right and responsibilities

Skills for democracy in action

References

Board of Education (1931) *The Primary School*. Report of the Consultative Committee (The Hadow Report). London: HMSO.

CBI (1989) *Towards a Skills Revolution*. London: Confederation of British Industry.

Centre for Contemporary Cultural Studies (1981) *Unpopular Education*. London: Hutchinson.

Commission on Citizenship (1990) *Encouraging Citizenship*. London: HMSO.

DES (1977) *Education in Schools. A Consultative Document*. London: HMSO.

DES (1985a) *Education for All* (The Swann Report). London: HMSO.

DES (1985b) *Better Schools*. London: HMSO.

Fogelman, K. (1990) 'Appendix', in *Encouraging Citizenship*. London: HMSO.

NCC (1989) *Curriculum Guidance No. 2: A Curriculum for All*. York: National Curriculum Council.

NCC (1990a) *Curriculum Guidance No 3: The Whole Curriculum*. York: National Curriculum Council.

NCC (1990b) *Curriculum Guidance No. 4: Education for Economic and Industrial Understanding*. York: National Curriculum Council.

NCC (1990c) *Curriculum Guidance No. 5: Health Education*. York: National Curriculum Council.

NCC (1990d) *Curriculum Guidance No. 6: Careers Education and Guidance*. York: National Curriculum Council.

NCC (1990e) *Curriculum Guidance No 7: Environmental Education*. York: National Curriculum Council.

NCC (1990f) *Core Skills 16–19*. York: National Curriculum Council.

Pike, G. and Selby, D. (1986) 'Global education', in Wellington J. J. (Ed.) *Controversial Issues in the Curriculum*. Oxford: Basil Blackwell.

Social and Community Planning Research (1989) *Talking About Commitment*. London: SCPR.

Ungoed Thomas, J. R. (1972) *Our School – A Handbook on the Practice of Democracy by Secondary School Pupils*. Harlow: Longman.

White, P. (1973) *Towards a Compulsory Curriculum*. London: Routledge and Kegan Paul.

White, P. (Ed.) (1989) *Personal and Social Education: Philosophical Perspectives*. London: The Bedford Way Press.

Wringe, C. (1984) *Democracy, Schooling and Political Education*. London: George Allen and Unwin.

CHAPTER 8

Citizenship Education

Val Lynch and Keith Smalley

Introduction

This chapter, written before the National Curriculum Council
published its detailed guidance on citizenship, tries to do two things.
First, it identifies, out of the practice of Leicestershire schools, the
major current components of citizenship education. It is suggested
that citizenship education might consist of four components:

- Developing knowledge and understanding concerning how our
  democratic society works, how it evolved, and our rights, duties and
  obligations. Within this would come the identification of concepts
  associated with citizenship such as equity, fairness and equality.
- Developing a respect for persons and developing fundamental sub-
  stantive and procedural values such as participation and consultation.
- Developing the skills of citizenship.
- Providing the experience of community and developing active citizenship within the community.

It is important to realize that any one component in isolation is
inadequate. 'Citizenship as a study area is particularly vulnerable
either to being presented as theory without practice, as in civic courses,
or to being offered solely as an experience, as practice without theory'
(Commission on Citizenship, 1990).

Second, the chapter offers case studies drawn from schools in
Leicestershire. They demonstrate the potential of specific activities to
embrace more than one component. There is no implied certainty or
complacency in the chapter; schools and colleges are dynamic and

developing institutions making more progress in some areas than others. The case studies illustrate how schools are approaching citizenship education because, whilst citizenship ideas have been current in educational thinking for over a century, schools are developing approaches more appropriate to the needs of society in the latter years of the twentieth century. This chapter gives some insights into the way Leicestershire schools are thinking about and responding to the challenge of implementing this particular cross-curricular theme. It should not be surprising that this chapter draws heavily on the work of the Report of the Speakers Commission on Citizenship with which Leicestershire was involved.

A body of knowledge and key understandings

According to T. H. Marshall (1950), being a citizen involves 'belonging to a community'. The most easily recognized community is the legally defined national community. Belonging to a community involves at a minimum an understanding of the framework of rules or guiding principles that govern that community. Whilst the family has an important role to play here, it is to the school that falls the major role for systematically teaching aspects of citizenship, for helping students understand how a democratic society works and how it evolves and for helping them recognize different cultures and values and the worth of each individual. School is generally where pupils first experience a sense of community.

In Leicestershire many teachers have been involved in developing an understanding of citizenship through Geography, History, Humanities courses, RE and Personal and Social Education courses and through thematic approaches in primary schools. Depending on the age and circumstances of the pupils and the particular situation of the school, students have been introduced to many of the topics suggested by international bodies:

- the main categories of human rights, duties, obligations and responsibilities
- the various forms of injustice, inequality and discrimination including sexism and racism
- people, movement and key events, both successses and failures, in the historical and continuing struggle for human rights
- the main international declarations and conventions of human rights (Council of Europe, 1985).

Students are introduced to these ideas in a positive and balanced way where the learning focuses on understanding for which knowledge is necessary, but is not the dominant consideration.

With the introduction of the National Curriculum core and foundation subjects, schools will have opportunities to address citizenship issues. The study of History will involve, for example, an understanding of how rights and liberties develop and how they may be threatened, and how in the UK the history of parliament involves the principle of government by consent. 'Through their history lessons pupils will learn that change is inherent in any democratic society and that democracy like freedom has to be won, is valuable, not perfectible, is valued beyond price and needs to be maintained and defended' (NCC, 1990a). History and Geography will also develop genuine international awareness and understanding necessary for the development of effective citizenship of the world.

The aim of such learning is to

> lead to an understanding of and sympathy for the concepts of justice, equality, freedom, place, dignity, rights and democracy. Such understanding should be both cognitive and based on experience and feelings. Schools should thus provide opportunities for pupils to experience effective involvement in human rights and to express their feelings through drama, art, music, creative writing and audio visual media (Council of Europe, 1985).

Schools do not find formal political education easy but students need a language of politics. They need to acquire an understanding of issues over which people disagree, a knowledge of groups involved in decision-making, an understanding of the processes and influence of local and central government. They will need to gain an understanding of the concepts used to categorize political knowledge and experience, including general political concepts such as authority, freedom, liberty; concepts associated with political machinery such as elections; concepts associated with beliefs and ideologies such as democracy; concepts associated with specific issues such as racism. Schools also need to encourage attitudes which are fundamental to responsible political activity: tolerance, open-mindedness, acceptance of compromise and personal responsibility as well as specific skills.

'Teachers should take care to avoid imposing their personal convictions on their pupils and involving them in ideological struggle' (Council of Europe, 1985). A previous generation of Leicestershire teachers would have used the Stenhouse neutral chairman approach as a pedagogic tool. Teachers today have appropriate strategies for dealing with controversial issues which allow them to fulfil the requirements of section 44 and 45 of the Education (No 2) Act of 1986 to offer students a balanced presentation of opposing views.

If citizenship education involves a body of knowledge and understandings the example of the Law in Education Project (SCDC, 1989) illustrates the importance of developing learning strategies which will involve students and so develop those understandings. Acknowledging the importance of the law in all aspects of our lives and the need for students to develop a concern for justice, social responsibility and the rights of others, the project produced materials designed to encourage the acquisition of knowledge and the development of understanding in a way which encourages students to see the purpose of the work and have an interest in the subject matter, appreciate the reasons for legislation and discuss the law for themselves as far as possible. A range of active learning strategies is employed to involve students in the learning process.

The materials have been used in Leicestershire in a variety of ways within Humanities courses, as modules within PSE courses and as a basis for modular courses within the Leicestershire Modular Framework, and accredited for GCSE. The emphasis given to a wide range of learning strategies, the use of visits and outside help and the encouragement of student talk in the classroom all aim to make complex ideas accessible to students of all abilities and to involve students in an appreciation of the issues introduced.

Further, if schools wish to help young people develop their personal autonomy and to live a purposeful life then schools need to help young people to learn effectively so that it becomes a life-long activity. Schools need to help young people to learn how to learn and to provide opportunities for them to learn through active involvement in the real world, applying and using knowledge. The Leicestershire review of community education and youth and community work has sensible things to say about learning in Leicestershire:

> The idea of a life long education is a powerful idea which has a relevance to education throughout a student's formal education. Managing one's own learning requires intrinsic motivation, planning and enquiry skills. Many of the current initiatives in Leicestershire schools are explicitly concerned with students managing their studies . . . (giving) students a greater sense of ownership of their own learning. Seeing students move towards a position of autonomy is a precursor to seeing life long education as a realistic goal for education beyond school (Clayton and Payne, 1988).

Many steps have been taken in the Leicestershire LEA to attempt to translate intention in to reality. Some of these steps have been associated with TVEI with which Leicestershire has been associated from its launch in 1983. The initiative then involved a relatively small number of students, but with the extension phase major curriculum developments affected all schools 14–19. Many of the aims of TVEI in Leicestershire have relevance to citizenship education.

'Respect for other people'

Citizenship education involves knowledge and understanding. Students develop their knowledge and understanding of the rights and duties of the individual in a social context. But it also involves the development of attitudes and values which underpin the notions of rights, duties and obligations. The school has a responsibility to contribute to the student's awareness of and respect for other people, other persons and their rights and duties. Respect is not used here to mean deference but in the more philosophical sense of 'respect for persons', the positive valuing of the personhood of others in their complex difference and similarity. Such valuing and mutual respect are not easily taught, nor are they easily and only acquired in a school setting. But the school is a community, or collection of communities, within which personal relationships develop. Students absorb values through the quality of the relationships experienced in and encouraged by a school community. These include the direct relationships between peers and between student and teacher and also the more indirect relationships between teacher and teacher, teacher and head teacher, teacher and support staff, staff and governors and parents all of which contribute to whole-school relationships, practices and the prevailing ethos.

Much has been written about the 'hidden curriculum' or those values which are transmitted to students through the kinds of relationships and practices which prevail in a school, which can enhance the dignity of the student or have a limiting effect. Small but important examples of such valuation can be seen in procedures like displaying students work on the wall, recognizing achievement through praise, displaying trust in students by giving them responsible tasks, turning up punctually for class and most importantly offering a curriculum that recognizes and values the contribution of all to a multicultural society. As the Council of Europe (1985) recommends, all students should be valued: 'Schools and teachers should attempt to be positive towards all their pupils and recognise that all their achievements are important – whether they be academic, artistic, musical, sporting or practical'. Consistency in relationships is important. From school surveys it seems that school policies concerning rules and sanctions are seen to be a significant factor in producing a cohesive community and dealing with anti-social behaviour. Some schools have involved students fully in devising codes of conduct or policies on particular issues such as bullying or graffiti. Some see it as important to limit written rules to a few simple guidelines which are understood to cover the detail of everyday life and thereby aim to encourage a sense of personal responsibility. Unsatisfactory behaviour can be dealt with in ways that indicate disapproval of the behaviour but maintain respect for the individual.

Valuing the person is perhaps most explicitly seen in the quality of guidance and pastoral care offered in a school. Tutorial group inter-actions, individual counselling, as well as informal conversation reveal the principles valued by the school and such demonstrations of respect for persons are likely to influence student behaviour. It must be said that assessment issues will need to be handled very sensitively if respect for persons is to be sustained.

Citizenship education will involve preparing students for adult roles and responsibilities. Schools will need to give to students the oppor-tunities to rehearse their adult roles, exercising some responsibility, engaging in democratic debate and making decisions, coping with the outcome, good or bad. It is not easy for a school to give students responsibility with the aim of developing pupil autonomy and yet, as Hargreaves (1984) puts it, exercise reasonable and reasoned control over behaviour. Some schools have found pupil, year and whole-school councils helpful. These differ in structure, organization, remit and powers but they are one way in which students can be given a degree of power and responsibility and the experience of democratic procedures. They encourage a growing awareness of the protocol of formal meetings, and encourage some research in to proposals as well as providing the learning experiences of presenting a case and possibly managing a small budget. It enables young people to have the confid-ence and ability to initiate debate and to organize and implement specific proposals in the implementation of change.

Schools are, thus, conscious of themselves as not only places where individuals achieve academic success but as places which should encourage citizenship education both in the sense of knowledge and understanding and through developing a respect for persons – a pre-requisite for participation in a democratic society. By developing as a community, schools can contribute greatly to this process. Within a community, social relations can develop which recognize the dignity of others and the groups to which they belong, build on mutual respect and help students to accept the same obligations. These are fundamental concerns of citizenship education.

Some schools would go further and, drawing on transatlantic ideas and practices, have a vision of the 'just school'. The just school would be concerned to develop students' understanding of justice and fairness. It would explicitly raise issues of fairness through cognitive moral dilemmas or discussion of issues within the school community. It would encourage role play and so enhance the student's capability to take the part of the other. It would consider fairness and morality. It would encourage active participation in group decision-making and exposure to higher levels of moral reasoning. The school would also be seen to *act* fairly, to value the views and perceptions of students; it would encourage students to take decisions and engage in democratic participation; it would encourage students to take responsibility for their own actions. Few schools at present would claim to be just schools but many would set this goal or vision to which they aspire. The 'just school' project in Leicestershire is in its infancy but its contribution to citizenship education may be judged from the case study given (No. 7, pp. 109–10).

The development of skills

The third component of citizenship education concerns the development and exercise of specific skills necessary for full participation in a democratic society.

Among the skills which have been identified as supporting citizenship are intellectual skills and social skills. There are the intellectual skills associated with written and oral expression, including the ability to listen and discuss and to defend one's opinions. There are skills involving judgement such as the collection and examination of material from various sources including the mass media, and the ability to analyse it and arrive at fair and balanced conclusions; the identification of bias, prejudice, stereotypes and discrimination. Students need to seek, question and evaluate a range of views and evidence; recognize slanted interpretation, exaggeration and bias; distinguish between fact and opinion; recognize reasons for the positions people adopt and the effects of certain courses of action. Students need to identify the choices open to them and establish the action they themselves with to pursue.

There is a variety of social skills which may be encouraged in school and which are necessary for effective participation in a democratic society. Students need to develop the capacity to debate, argue and present a coherent point of view. They need to recognize and accept differences and establish positive and non-oppressive personal relationships. They need to resolve conflict in a non-violent way. They need to take responsibility by representing others, for example on a school council. They need to work collaboratively and work as a member of a team. They need to be able to protest, for example by writing to a newspaper or councillor or local store. The development of social, planning, organizational, negotiating and debating skills is important. 'Young people should leave school with some confidence in their ability to participate in their society, to resolve conflict and if they oppose a course of action, to express that opposition fairly, effectively and peacefully' (Commission on Citizenship, 1990).

It is interesting to note what the final report of the Geography Working Group for the National Curriculum had to say about citizenship:

> A competent citizen should be able to recognise situations and contexts where power and authority are in operation, appreciate resulting issues, know who is affected and how, be able to understand and if necessary participate in decision making, be capable of identifying and taking action and be able to evaluate the implications of taking such action (NCC, 1990b).

Many schools are involved in such activities as environmental improvements or environmental investigations which inevitably involve students in all of the skills identified. As one principal of a 14–19 Leicestershire college put it:

> Our students have engaged in a wide range of activities. Active citizenship includes enabling young people to have the confidence and ability to initiate debate, organise around, and implement specific proposals in the implementation of change. In a community college setting the attitude of adults is crucial. One of the preconditions seems to be that students are assumed to be responsible, sensitive and capable of independent decision making and that adults are supportive of students' activities and seen to be involved themselves. Activities rather than laborious committee structures are initially more effective. The many skills involved in sustaining committee structures need to be learnt over time and might evolve from the activities.

Active voluntary participation in the wider community

A variety of active associations and organizations are the key to a healthy participatory democracy. More and more people are actively involved in a whole series of common concerns. People contribute to a democratic community in a variety of ways: they raise funds and care for dependent relatives; they contribute through independent voluntary organizations and political parties; they contribute to communities at different levels, locally and nationally. There are communities of adversity (such as Neighbourhood Watch). Public services increasingly work in partnership with community groups on particular projects. Public sources are increasingly using volunteers. There is increased involuntary participation – the many 'carers' in our society. The role of independent voluntary bodies is increasing. There are many advantages in such developments, benefits both for the individual and the society but equally there are many disadvantages. What is needed is a balance between individual service and public service and private provision and voluntary service.

What is clear is that 'the voluntary contribution by individual citizens to the common good through the participation and exercise of civic duty and the encouragement of such activities by public and private institution is a part of citizenship' (Commission on Citizenship, 1990). As a society we need to broaden the involvement of citizens. It follows that schools should help students develop the knowledge, understanding, skills and values to enable them effectively to contribute to that plural participating society. Thus, experience within the community is important for the individual as an encouragement to make a contribution in later life. The study of citizenship involves learning democratic behaviour from the experience of the school as an institution playing a role in the wider community. As the Speaker puts it:

> Young people at the outset of their adult lives need to be offered the experience of working with others to tackle and solve real problems in their own local environment. I believe that experience of involvement, of belonging, of sharing responsibility is a crucial element in the process of learning to be a good citizen (Commission on Citizenship, 1990).

The survey of citizenship activities in Leicestershire and Northamptonshire schools showed the variety of current community activity. Many students are involved with visiting or helping people, the elderly, the disabled, the ill and children, and working for voluntary or statutory services or bodies, on environmental projects or charity work. These are common factors of schools across the age range, with perhaps older students showing greater activity.

It would be surprising if community activities were not well developed in an Authority with a long tradition of life-long comprehensive community education. The 36 community colleges and 35 primary-based community centres combine variously within a single and integrated institution the functions of a school, an adult education centre, an arts centre, a youth centre, a sports and social centre and provide a wide range of specialist functions for social and recreational faculties for all ages. There are major debates of policy within community education: whether community education should be complementary to school provision – something added on to and growing naturally out of existing school provision – or should its distinguishing task be to effect a change in the community, a change in the relationship and attitudes which enable people themselves to improve the quality of life and create opportunities and demands which the education service might meet. Schools which are community colleges or centres may be influenced by these debates and staff develop their educational philosophies within them. In many cases staff will be concerned to promote educational activities that are related to the life experience of the learner, validate the social experience of the child and incorporate it within the texture of learning. Schools will use the community as a resource. They will develop close links with industry and with other community-based organizations, agencies and services. This is the context within which much citizenship education occurs, in the relationship between a school and its local community.

In the view of the NCC (1990c) a component of citizenship education is 'work and employment', an understanding of rights and duties, employment legislation, trade unions, economic factors affecting employment, and wealth generation. Much of the knowledge and associated understandings in this area will be acquired and developed across the whole curriculum but many of the skills relevant to adult life and employment and many of the attitudes are often best developed through partnership activities with business and the wider community. Many students supported by TVEI developments are actively involved within their local communities: work experience is seen as part of the core entitlement of students. Within the city is the Leicester Compact initiative, and the Work Experience Agency. Links with industry have meant that students have engaged in a wide variety of experiences: subject- or theme-based links involving learners in problem-solving in real life situations, work shadowing, community work experience, careers visits, industry days, and industrial tutors. Link courses with FE have been integrated within a student's total programme. Most importantly the students develop knowledge, understanding, skills and attitudes which are not only relevant to adult working life and employment but also skills, maturity and motivation which are essential to participatory membership of a wider democratic community.

There is little space to detail the range of community placements, and the benefits of welcoming the community to the school. Nor is this the place to develop the theme that community is not merely the local, some would say the parochial, but involves wider continental and global considerations. Visits to centres in France and Germany and to other parts of Europe not only help students to develop their linguistic competence but add a European Community dimension to students' thought. Direct global experience is more limited but fund raising and school links with African and South American countries provide some basis for developing skills, values and attitudes towards global citizenship ideas. By itself each activity might appear to be limited but in combination they extend horizons, encourage participation and predispose students to contribute to the common good.

The school exists within a series of wider communities. In a society with a healthy democratic tradition the importance of the voluntary contribution of citizens to their own society is recognized and encouraged. The school should, through its arrangements and relationships, foster the development of the empowerment of the individual within his or her community. A mature democratic society welcomes participation.

Conclusion

This chapter has explored the components of citizenship education. What is clear is that schools face an exciting challenge in introducing all the facets of such an important area of the curriculum. Many schools have made major advances in particular activities and initiatives as our case studies demonstrate. But all schools would recognize that more needs to be done before it can be said that all students leave school with a predisposition to be active citizens of a participatory democracy. Much thought needs to be given to the creation of a broad and coherent approach to citizenship education and much thought needs to be given to issues of implementation.

Along with the other cross curricular themes it will need to be given some priority in the curriculum review and have a place in school development plans.

It is unlikely that schools will wish to timetable each cross-curricular theme separately. Much of the work associated with the themes will permeate the core and foundation subjects and through themes and any separately timetabled events. There may, occasionally, be a block of time given over to such citizenship activities as community involvement and elections. The provision of experiences promoting citizenship cannot be left to chance and will need to be systematically planned.

Citizenship studies and experience will be part of each student's entitlement. Achievement in this area needs to be recognized. Many schools in Leicestershire, as nationally, have developed records of achievement where achievements may be celebrated.

'Citizenship, whatever it means, is a cultural achievement, a gift of history which can be lost or destroyed' (Commission on Citizenship, 1990). Schools can lay solid foundations but active citizenship is, like education, something for life. Citizenship should be an integral part of every young person's education; schools will respond to the guidance of the NCC and the messages of this book and give the theme the weight it deserves within the planned experience offered to the student.

CASE STUDIES

Case study 1: Burleigh College (14–19), Loughborough

The College is typical of many Community Colleges in Leicestershire offering in-house projects like the crèche, playgroup, frail and elderly day care, adult groups for people with special needs, youth clubs, lunch clubs.

Normally, students would be placed on a project at certain times of the week and act as an extra body to help. The 'Community in Mind' project goes further; it aims to give young people real participation in planning and organizing and real involvement in community work. It is offered to students following the College's alternative curriculum. They work together as a group and agree to service each project continuously. They plan timetables to ensure each project is adequately staffed. They participate in relevant committee work and one is a member of the College Management Committee. They plan new projects and new services (from gardening in the campus to teaching swimming to local primary children). They run a conference service (welcoming members, ushering, catering) and a publicity service (printing, folding, delivering publicity). They arrange one-off projects such as the Community Bonfire Party, a Christmas Dinner for the frail and elderly and a mobile disco.

Students, often previously 'disaffected' and with poor attendance records, through active involvement with others, refine their understanding of personal responsibility and develop attitudes which are prerequisites for participatory citizenship over their lifetime. Decision-making and negotiation skills are developed in a real, involving context. 'I liked it because we weren't told what to do. We made decisions jointly and everyone was equal and had real responsibilities'.

The concept of 'learning for life' has encouraged teachers to plan and negotiate experiences which start from 'where the student is at' to a longer-term view beyond College. The knowledge and understanding which need to be acquired arise from the experience which has been planned with the student. In order to be successful, new skills or more complicated skills need to be practised. This process of individualizing learning experiences is not new to teachers who prepare students for the foundation programmes of BTEC. They become a preparation for citizenship because they focus on achievement which depends on a student's developing relationship with other people.

Case study 2: Castle Rock High School

Castle Rock is a Leicestershire high school (11–14) near Coalville. One way it is able to approach citizenship education is through an 'Applied Studies' integrated afternoon. Eighteen different courses are offered at any one time and last for six weeks. All Applied Studies courses are derived from – and are intended to develop and enhance – the formal curriculum. Knowledge and understanding, therefore, form an integral part of citizenship education.

The Applied Studies idea is founded on the broad conviction that via their organization and expectation, schools can tap into and enhance the maturing process in pupils to bring broad personal/educational advantage. In short, pupils are placed in a series of challenging situations; they develop a wide range of skills – not normally expected of young people – which enables them to respond in a mature and effective manner.

The active involvement of local industry with this curriculum development has been encouraged by setting up an Industrial Support Group consisting of industrialists willing to contribute their time and expertise. Dunlop staff have helped to develop technological aspects of the curriculum; Bardon Quarries provided a pond now used as a basis for a business project; Ibstock Brick organized a teaching module involving the design of a brick seat; in conjunction with the EMEB students are monitoring the construction of energy-efficient bungalows for elderly people. Another activity involves students in monitoring the restoration work at Snibston Mine (a coal mining and technology museum) and producing a photographic record.

The integrated afternoon provides opportunities for activities which help those with mental handicaps at a local school, research the difficulties the elderly face concerning mobility and access within the community, and offer help to the old people's hospital. Conversations with local old people are used for oral history. The 'reading for the blind' activity has grown into a regular 20-minute radio programme.

The construction, planning and implementation of these optional courses – by the nature of the various processes – demand and evoke a request for others and other views. This a key issue, whether at the early pupil-planning meetings which are a pre-requisite for some courses, or when pupils are working alongside adults, who may or may not be teachers.

The school aims to establish a curriculum 'truly and fully owned by the community'. The community is perceived as a resource (while it is encouraged to view the school in the same way) and as a partner. It is in the Applied Studies area of the curriculum that this partnership of responsibility is most effectively achieved. While pupils acquire their own perceptions of the interdependence of school and community, and realize their own central part in the process, they truly begin their citizenship education.

Case study 3: Beauchamp College, Oadby

Beauchamp College is a Leicestershire Upper School and Community College (14–19). Some teachers in the RE department use 'contracts' as a tool for education and citizenship. Six lessons are used to create positive relationships in the classroom; activities include introduction, listening skills, put-downs, push-ups, brainstorming, stereotyping, looking at what really helps us learn and drawing up a contract. The class brainstorms 'How can we help each other learn in this class?' and draws up agreements for a *class contract*. (Only the last agreement in this contract for 14–15 year olds came from the teacher).

4d Partnership Contract

1. Cooperate with each other.
2. Listen to each other (don't speak when someone is talking to the whole class).
3. Help each other.
4. Don't distract people.
5. Be able to say what you think honestly without being put down/laughed at.
6. Don't leave people out.
7. Help each other be confident.
8. No sarcastic comments.
9. Work towards a GCSE in RE.

Signed _____   date _____

Each line is agreed democratically by consensus if possible, and the whole contract voted on. The accepted contract is copied and signed by each student and the teacher.

> Students by and large welcome it. Those who put up resistance have to deal more with peer pressure than with me. The contract helps make clear the values and norms of the class so that students know where they are with each other and with me, the teacher. Since these are negotiated, the students take ownership and responsibility to keep the spirit of the contract.
>
> I find that if I work on relationships at the beginning, the exam work will look after itself. Working at good classroom relationships and a sense of direction through a negotiated contract increases student productivity and motivation . . . . The greatest dividend is satisfying relationships because trust is growing.

Exam results are well above average.

An *individual 'contract'* is used for an assignment on some religious or moral question. The student chooses the question from a list on the topic being studied, or makes up his or her own and negotiates with me, the teacher. Guidelines are given on planning but how the student plans the use of time, research, and writing his or her answer is up to the individual student. There is just a final deadline, given 5 weeks or so before. In the particular course we do, using Beliefs and Values GCSE modules from the Leicestershire modular framework, this individual contract forms the evidence for the planning skill which is awarded marks and counts towards the final GCSE grade. This individual contract enables students to plan and in a sense contract not so much with me, but with themselves individually.

Student reaction? I am always amazed at the real sense of ownership of the task by most students right across the ability range. There is a significant rise in productivity and the meeting of the final deadline.

Contracts in the classroom are a way of the teacher sharing power and responsibility with students. The result is an empowerment of the student which results in an increase in motivation and productivity. Perhaps most importantly the teacher has enabled students to participate democratically in their own learning, individually and collectively. These classroom contracts also help students learn practically the values and skill of citizenship, the values and skills at the heart of our democratic society. Negotiated contracts balance freedom with responsibility! Since the Bible describes even God doing this, shouldn't RE teachers at least try? And maybe every other teacher in the land!

A booklet: *Contracts* has been produced giving detailed plans of the six introductory lessons leading up to a class contract, the use of individual contracts, an evaluation of student response and a discussion of theoretical principles. It can be obtained from Beauchamp College, Oadby, LE2 5TP.

Case study 4: Hamilton Community College (11–16), Leicester

Year 8 students at Hamilton studied the local community as part of a co-ordinated PSE, tutorial and Humanities programme. They aimed to identify groups in the community with particular needs. They designed and implemented surveys and found that 'some groups (the elderly housebound) were disenfranchized and needed help'. (They needed a local chemist, would benefit from groceries and appreciate personal contact, particularly having their reminiscences valued). The students aimed to respond to these needs. They raised funds; they raised peer awareness through sketches in assembly; they planned suitable purchases, designed gift packaging; they produced a booklet of reminiscences. As an outcome a local MP was invited to hear the case for a local pharmacy – now there is a chemist in the community. Pupils organized presents of groceries to the elderly, and learned much local history from oral reminiscences.

An analysis of this activity would suggest that it provides opportunities for students developing this knowledge and understanding of the local community, and clarifying concepts of rights and duties and acquiring information about local political processes. The students were responding to real community needs and in becoming real agents for change developed an empathetic understanding, valuing the experience of others. They developed study, interviewing, listening, talking and report-writing skills. They developed self-reliance, trust and responsibility for decisions and actions.

The necessary conditions for this activity included willing collaboration between staff teams, involvement of senior management, coordination of tasks and giving students responsibility to evaluate the local environment as a starting point. This is just one aspect of 'citizenship' education implemented at the college.

Staff at the college recognize the aspects of citizenship that are concerned with a body of knowledge and understanding and have emphasized them in their own right, as well as being part of themes within Humanities. This case study demonstrates clearly the 'respect for others' dimension of citizenship and the college works hard to develop an ethos that re-affirms this on many occasions. It is possible to identify 'skills for citizenship' in many aspects of the curriculum which reinforce the work done in PSE or tutorial time. As a Community College, events and activities that involve students with members of the community are commonplace both within the formal and informal curriculum.

Case study 5: Lutterworth Grammar School and Community College

The school is a large 14–19 Leicestershire upper school with many school activities contributing to citizenship education.

One tutor group project involved year 10 students raising money to finance a Christmas Party for the frail and elderly (35 over-80s). Money was raised by cooking flans, cakes, etc. for sale within the school. Samples of the food to be sold were made first and advertised in the school bulletin. Orders were taken. The items were sold at lunch-times and after school. A delivery system was also arranged. £500 profit resulted. The second part of the project involved contacting Age Concern to arrange a list of guests and provide transport. Students designed invitations and planned menus, using the word processor. They made individual visits to the homes of the guests. They decorated the party room, provided taped music, and arranged for a photographer. They cooked the meal, served drinks, waited at tables and assisted with mobility. They ran a raffle including the collection of prizes from townspeople. The project was planned in tutor group time and executed in the pupils' own time.

Subsequently, the group entered their project for the Spirit of Enterprise Award Scheme, sponsored by the National Westminster Bank plc within their 'Community Enterprise' Project. In winning the National Award, the group received a cheque for £2000 at a special presentation in London for school equipment. However, the group elected to invest a proportion of the money to provide funds for the regular future entertainment of senior citizens. Such events, often coinciding with school Drama and Music events, are now regular features in the school calendar.

Case study 6: Moat Community College, Leicester

Moat Community College is an 11–16 inner-city school with students from a wide range of ethnic backgrounds. Year 9 students are engaged in a ten-week module on racism as part of a PSE Programme, building on year 8 work on Equal Opportunities. The aim of each module (1 hour per week) is to reflect the needs of the community within which the school is situated and help students develop their skills in dealing with racism. The course is planned by the head of PSE at Moat and staff from the authority's multicultural centre. It explores how racism has developed, how it manifests itself today and how people can, do and should challenge it. It emphasizes black achievement. The learning revolves around a video input, discussion, role play, questionnaire, structured worksheets, reflection and recording of thoughts.

The course contributes to 'The pursuit of equality, including equality of educational opportunity, through the combating of racism and the elimination of discrimination' (LCC, 1985). The aim is to:

(a) provide an opportunity to explore 'black achievement' and its importance, both historically and in the present day;
(b) prepare all students to live and work harmoniously and with equality of opportunity in a multicultural society;
(c) build on the strengths of cultural diversity in that society;
(d) define and combat racism and any discriminatory practice within the education service to which it gives rise;
(e) meet appropriately the particular educational needs of all people 'having regard to their ethnic, cultural, linguistic or historical attachment'.

The course relates at a number of levels with the four aspects of citizenship with reference to inequality, discrimination, racism and the issue of human rights.

Case study 7: Millfield Primary School and Community College, Leicester

I shall describe, in broad terms, a regular school activity which encouraged key understandings and skill development associated with citizenship. It also embraces the central principle of 'respect for other people' and illustrates the merging of theory and practice in citizenship education.

Principally, through the work of Piaget and Kohlberg, I have become very interested in children's developing understanding of fairness and justice. I am also curious about how this understanding might enable pupils to actively participate in making their school a 'just community'. In following my interest, and in the hope of making our school more just, I decided to try to rationalize a process which had already gained a strong informal momentum.

It became clear to me that children wanted to use our daily school assemblies as a forum to express views about perceived unfairness resulting from pupil inter-action. Such expression gave rise to much animated discussion and tremendous interest. I decided to go with the flow and hand over some assemblies to the pupils for them to air their concerns; with certain rules:

Most important, all contributions should be respectful and respected.
Accusations related to perceived unfairness should be supported by evidence.
Views about perceived unfairness should be confirmed by reasoned argument.
Anyone accused of unfairness has the immediate right to reply.
We should all try to think how to stop unfair actions or events from occurring again.
The fact that someone has done an unfair thing does not mean that she or he

stops being a person and stops deserving respect (everyone is capable of
doing good or bad things).

Some issues may be too sensitive to discuss in assembly, but the notion of open
debate concerning issues of fairness and justice should be seen as very
important.

I shall listen very carefully to pupils' ideas about how their school can be made
more just, but I reserve the right to accept, modify or reject such ideas.

Most pupils appear to best understand these rules through their practice, but
it is important that they are often stated to remind us when rational
discussion is degenerating into an exchange of prejudices.

Assemblies are not ideal situations for allowing everyone to contribute to
discussions, but they do provide regular opportunities for all pupils to see
that their perceptions of fairness and justice are taken seriously. They also
place the perpetrators of injustice under the revealing and cautionary light of
an open forum.

Active participation in the making of fairness and justice is the substance
of moral development. Pupils who know that they can readily and effectively
discuss justice as it relates to them will also be emotionally more free to
respond to other aspects of the school's curriculum.

The just school is open, creative and productive. Have I defined 'loving'?

Case study 8: Greenacres School, Leicester

Greenacres is an all-age special school in Leicestershire taking statemented
students who have moderate learning difficulties. Individual programmes in
the lower school aim to develop basic skills and boost self-esteem. In the
senior section these skills are used in modular courses and in real world
situations, in the community, in child care and in leisure activities. The
curriculum is orientated towards the outside world through links with local
schools, business and industry and with the community.

Community links are embedded in the curriculum. Pupils use community
facilities (outdoor pursuits centre, libraries) and try to give something back
to the community. In a module lasting 12 weeks, the first few weeks are used
discussing the needs of the elderly, the handicapped, young children and
identifying and planning what the students can do to help. Students are
consulted about placements. Some help at an old people's home, or at the
neighbouring school for SLD students, others help caretakers at a secondary
school or the ground staff at Western Park, still others help within the school
(helping the secretary, caretakers, kitchen staff, reception class).

Work experience, community placements and work shadowing are
common. Additionally, as members of the Leicester Compact the school
maintains links with the local industry. A recent project involved the school
and a local firm using CAD to create designs for jumpers. Another link was
with British Shoe where pupils were involved in a project to promote the
company's centenary year and took part in an industrial day to explore what

companies expected of their employees. A largely photographic record of achievement celebrates student achievement.

This case study makes clear that all students are citizens and are capable of making useful contributions to the community. An entitlement curriculum needs to offer the opportunity for all students to develop the four aspects of citizenship education.

Case study 9: Rushey Mead School, Leicester

A tutor group in year 3 prepared to host a visit from a group of German students from the Saarland. The emphasis was on involving the students from Rushey Mead in planning, participating in and evaluating the link. They negotiated a programme of activities including considering the local environment and places of interest and anticipating what experiences the German students would value. They decided that to participate in joint activities would be most worthwhile and planned to share experiences in Drama and Graphics, not normally found in German schools' timetables. They helped plan the lesson. They planned and organized a barbeque and a visit to London. They planned how best to meet new people, imagining how the visitors might feel. During the visit a group of students video recorded the activities. Problems that were encountered were put back to the students for solutions and their ingenuity in problem-solving was outstanding. On reflection on the visit they identified that they had learned that although there are differences between cultures there are many similarities. They recognized the value of learning another language. They learnt the importance of planning, consultation and negotiation in achieving a successful event.

In relation to the theme of citizenship we can recognize from this example the potential, if offered, for recognizing responsibilities, particularly responsibilities towards guests in our country. The young people involved clearly could recognize the commitment that they and their school had entered into. There is also, in such a visit, the opportunity to challenge stereotyping and discrimination. In terms of skills that can be developed through such activity we can identify planning, negotiating, compromising, reflecting, empathizing, communicating, recognizing and valuing similarities and differences, problem-solving – the list could go on. The 'respect of persons' dimension of citizenship is no doubt at the heart of such an experience and it offers a real opportunity to learn about other's background, points of view, experiences and culture. It can be far more than a 'hosting' experience.

112

References

Clayton, G. and Payne, B. (1988) 'Community education in Leicestershire', *Community Education Review.*

Commission on Citizenship (1990) *Encouraging Citizenship.* Report of the Commission on Citizenship. London: HMSO.

Council of Europe (1985) 'Recommendation No R(85)7 of the Committee of Ministers to member states on Teaching and Learning about Human rights in schools'. Strasbourg: Council of Europe.

Hargreaves, D. (1984) *Improving Secondary Schools.* London: ILEA.

LCC (1985) *Working Party on Multicultural Education.* Leicester: Leicester-shire County Council.

LEA (1990) *Leicestershire Modular Framework.* An evaluation by J. Noble, J. Sykes amd J. Edwards. Leicester: Leicestershire Education Authority.

Marshall, T. H. (1950) *Citizenship and Social Class.* Cambridge: Cambridge University Press.

NCC (1990a) *History in the National Curriculum.* York: National Curriculum Council.

NCC (1990b) *Geography 5–16 in the National Curriculum.* York: National Curriculum Council.

NCC (1990c) *Curriculum Guidance No. 8: Education for Citizenship.* York: National Curriculum Council.

SCDC (1989) *Law Education Project: Using the Law.* London: Edward Arnold.

CHAPTER 9

Citizenship in Schools: A Political Perspective

Andrew Rowe MP

Esau sold his birthright for a mess of pottage. He knew what he was doing in the technical sense that he knew what the words meant but it is clear that he had no idea of what his transaction really implied. We have to ask whether our schoolchildren have any better idea of what is meant by citizenship. Why? Because in this century of all centuries we have seen millions and millions of grown men and women sell their citizenship for what has turned out to be an extreme of terror, cruelty and death. Ignorant of what it means to be a citizen in a democracy, the peoples of countries as diverse as Russia, Germany or Iran exchanged the fragile and complex network of rights and obligations which citizenship entails, for the tempting but ultimately fatal simplicities of ideology. There is nothing whatever to give us the assurance that it could not happen again or even that Britain's people would not go down the same route. It is easy to see that with every new dictatorship the techniques for ensuring its success grow ever more effective and one day we may find ourselves subjected to a dictatorship so overwhelming that it can resist decay for generations. That is the first reason why it is essential to make sure that children understand what it means to be a citizen.

But there are other reasons, too. If it is true that one purpose of education is to enable children to make the most of their capacities, no one can ignore the value of giving children responsibility while they are young enough for their mistakes to be contained in an environment

114

where the damage is limited and it is easy to learn from them. It is one thing to know what it means to be a citizen, another to have the chance to put the knowledge into practice. Schools have an unrivalled opportunity to provide that chance. Some of them do; most do not. I shall argue later that it is not necessary to confine that chance to the schools; there are plenty of opportunities waiting to be exploited outside. Only if children are given real responsibilities will they learn to value themselves and thus provide a bastion for themselves and others against tyrants, whose first move is always to undermine the individual's sense of worth.

Citizenship concerns both a description of someone's status and the ways in which people interact with one another. Both are of fundamental importance. As a status, citizenship is a passport to a host of entitlements. In the world as it is presently organized, citizenship within the European community is a passport to such a disproportionately rich set of entitlements that it seems improbable that the imbalance between them and those enjoyed by most of the world's citizens can be preserved at its present level for much longer, even if it were thought to be appropriate to try.

These are not empty or theoretical points. They are central to the debate over how the world is to develop in the next century and no one has a more immediate interest in that than those who are at school today or will shortly enter it.

The questions which children need to consider in each succeeding generation include the following: Are the bases on which we admit people to British citizenship appropriate and adequate? Does it, for example, make sense that Britain should be one of a few countries which make no demands on their citizens that they learn to speak the national language? Are they affected by the treaties and other international agreements which Britain has signed in recent years? If so, how? And do the new obligations secure for Britain and the rest of the European Community secure and morally justifiable bases for citizenship? (What we cannot ignore is that the rules which allow one person to become a citizen are the rules which simultaneously deny to millions that right). One of the great battles which will be fought out in the next century will be that between the 'haves', who will want to use their citizenship laws to avoid having to share with the 'have nots', and those who will seek to undermine the careful structures of national citizenship in order to increase their chance of achieving a share in the greater prosperity which they see accruing to those called citizens in prosperous countries. Only if citizens themselves have a clear idea about what it means to be a citizen will the debate have any chance of clarity. I do not pretend that clarity will necessarily ensure a generous response; it may well decrease the chance of generosity rather than increase it.

Yet, if we need to teach what is meant by citizenship in the international context, so that British children may know what British citizenship entails and can debate whether it is appropriately defined, we must also teach it in the national context. This is because, as the Speaker's Commission has pointed out, there exist serious inequities whose effect in many cases is to exclude British citizens from the exercise of their citizenship in all its scope.

This, too, is a debate which is central to the national political debate, because it goes to the heart of the arguments about the welfare state. At their simplest, these take the form of asserting that if the welfare state were better endowed and more fairly administered no one would be prevented by poverty and other misfortunes from exercising any of their rights as a citizen. Every politician knows that this is over simple. Many of the constituents who come to their Member's surgery show themselves as people who only have the time and energy to pursue their rights as a citizen because they have so little else to occupy them. And the phenomenon of the unemployed full-time political activist casts doubt on the simpler form of the welfare/citizenship argument. Yet, there is no doubt that there is an important argument to be debated here and we cannot shut our eyes to the social component in citizenship. Justice, for example, is no justice if delay or lack of financial resources prevent access to it.

Anyone who needs convincing that the debate about the status of citizens goes to the heart of matters with which school children are concerned has only to look at the current passionate debate about ethnic minority schools. In many parts of Britain parents are taking decisions about their children's schooling based on their position in that debate. It brings into sharp relief the frailty of the consensus about the status of citizens in a changing world. Is it indeed necessary for sectarian schools to be multiplied in a country which has already paid a high price for sectarianism in order to secure the effective rights of a British citizen? Would it be better to abolish those sectarian schools which already exist? Would it be practicable to do so? Only a population which has some understanding of what citizenship means can hope to deal rationally with such strongly emotional issues.

Not just a status

Citizenship is not only a status, although it is perfectly acceptable for any citizen to choose to regard it simply as such. As Ralph Dahrendorf argued to the Commission, it is dangerous and philosophically mistaken to argue that because citizens enjoy rights and incur obligations the two are reciprocal. If every citizen rejected every obligation of citizenship, to take part in elections, for example, every citizen would lose an important part of his or her rights but there is no obligation on every citizen always to take part in an election.

Citizenship is also a process, like growing up, and it is demonstrably possible to improve both one's contribution as a citizen and the quality of the benefit which one derives from being a citizen by actively working to do so. One of the papers submitted to the Speaker's Commission was called 'Active Citizenship and a Healthy Society' by David Halpern of the University of Cambridge. He argued that it is possible for individuals to improve their own capacity to succeed as individuals by actively working to serve others and that their ability to so improve increased if the work they did for others was carefully designed so as to be of effective service to them. In other words 'If carefully set up and fostered, active citizenship can be beneficial at all levels. The "activists" can gain, the "recipients" can gain, and the wider society can be shown to gain too'.

Halpern drew on research which examined the attitudes and 'loci of control' of 78 volunteer mental health workers before and after a three-month period of voluntary work at a State Mental Institution. The idea of the 'locus of control' is that some people perceive that the outcomes in their life are contingent on what he or she does ('internal') while others believe that events in their life are determined more by luck or powerful others than by themselves. Such 'externals' are far more likely to view themselves negatively and are more likely to develop depression. Miller compared 78 students who were doing voluntary work with 78 who were not. At the end of the three-month period, the volunteers had become significantly more internal in their locus of control than were the control group; this difference did not exist pre-test. One of the most exciting findings was that the students developed more favourable attitudes to the mentally ill with whom they were working. This fits in well with other studies (and indeed the experience of many projects in many different countries) that working with different groups reduces considerably the prejudices hitherto felt about the groups. If the modern world is to stand any chance of breaking down the hostilities which exist between races, religions, and other groupings we have to provide opportunities for people to work alongside the groups to which they feel instinctively hostile.

The devastating success of tyrants like Stalin and Hitler in using prejudice, based largely on the fear born of ignorance, to establish their tyrannies and to maintain them should warn us all of the urgent need to develop strategies for enabling citizens of every age, but perhaps particularly the young, to test their prejudices against reality. Only if citizens can bond together will our generation avoid the appalling fragmentation which allowed millions to be slaughtered because when every man is an island no man's death diminishes him. It is, however, vital that active citizens set out to help groups other than their own. Otherwise, as Halpern (1990) says, 'if active citizenship just means helping one's own group, then selfishness is not removed; it's just that selfish and competing individuals come to be replaced by selfish and competing groups'.

The Council of Europe takes the matter equally seriously as its Recommendation No. R(85)7 makes clear. It has recommended that both human rights and democracy be taught actively throughout the schools in member countries.

There is another reason why all of us have an interest in encouraging active citizenship. The disproportionate increase in the number of the elderly and infirm, accompanied by a notable falling off in the number of young people in the population, means that there will be an unparalleled need for volunteers to help share the load of caring for people who can no longer care entirely for themselves. Studies show that people who have volunteered when they are young are more likely to volunteer when they are older. It is, therefore, important to take seriously the proposals in the Commission's report for building into the educational recognition system experience and achievements gained as volunteers at school. It seems very unlikely that, in a period when the demands on curricular time are increasing, children and their teachers will be able to set aside time for community and other altruistic projects if they are not afforded recognition in the system of educational validation. It seems to be self-evident that experience gained in organizing and delivering care or in protecting the environment calls for the exercise of qualities the development of which are usually claimed to lie at the heart of a school's strategy for its pupils. The Fogelman (1990) study showed that an encouraging number of schools are using this sort of experience to improve their reporting on their pupils but it will certainly help if this is carried over into the national validation procedure.

It is, however, a mistake to confine to school life strategies for encouraging the young to take citizenship actively. At this point we should confront an uncomfortable paradox. Every year we prolong pupillage for ever more children as we try to prepare them for an increasingly technological society. At the same time, we perpetuate our old attitudes toward students and give out the message that while they may, if they wish, play some direct part in running student affairs, any attempt to break into running the wider society outside the student fence will be made boring and/or difficult. In this way, we manage both to cut the power structures of our society off from the talents, energy and innovativeness of the young and to breed a lack of interest in how society is managed which will cost us dear in future years.

Yet, paradoxically, political parties, trade unions, churches and other institutions all claim to be desperate to attract and keep young members. We need to look hard at this apparent contradiction. Why is it that the slice of the population with least ties and most energy takes so little part in running the society which it is shortly to inherit? I believe that it is partly because they have usually had far too little scope to discover how simple and rewarding it is to get involved. Some schools do try to give their pupils a genuine role in the formulation and execution of policy. Indeed, it was striking to see the very high numbers of schools in both the Fogelman (1990) study and that of Vlaeminke and Burkimsher (Chapter 5) which had pupil involvement in school councils and other bodies. We were not told what that entailed, but it is clear that the intention already exists in most schools. How many local authorities, however, have any mechanism for finding out what their younger constituents feel or want? As far as I know, none of them have a budget for young people to apply to any of the problems for which the authority takes responsibility. Would it not make sense for local authorities and other public institutions to look at some of the problems with which they grapple ineffectively (vandalism and litter are two inevitable examples) and then establish a young people's policy group to consider them? It would have to be understood that if any potential solution emerged some resources would be put aside to allow the young themselves to try putting their policy into effect. It has been shown that engagement without empowerment can actually foster, rather than reduce, an individual's sense of helplessness. Our resolute refusal to give the young any serious responsibility for the society in which they live merely encourages the kind of anomie which undermines citizenship, and we should change our ways.

Democracy as a presupposition

It is perfectly possible for someone to be a full citizen of his or her state without that state being in any sense a democracy. Indeed, it is common for governments, particularly those which feel threatened by the traditional organization of the people over whom they rule, to create a *de facto* citizenship which has little or nothing to do with tradition. Sometimes the citizenship has more than one tier. Thus, after the Russian revolution, the leaders of the new state, notably Stalin, set out to create forms of citizenship which depended not simply on place of birth, family descent or even tradition which have been the criteria often used to establish citizenship, but on such arbitrary criteria as usefulness to the government. It was dressed up as membership of the Party and other such categories but the truth was that effective citizenship became a gift from the government and could be taken away as easily as it was awarded. When this was reinforced with a whole hierarchy of privileges, in none of which the individual was allowed to establish a freehold, the power of the state to dominate and exploit its citizens became absolute. As a result, it became possible for the government to commit almost any form of crime against its subjects without any effective restraint.

For British citizens the position is sharply different. In the first place, many of their rights are freehold rights. An increasing number of Britons own property to which their rights are secured by both law and custom. They also can claim certain traditional protections, such as their rights under habeas corpus, which can only be suspended in times of emergency. Yet, as many authorities have pointed out, sometimes, like Enoch Powell, approvingly and sometimes, like Lord Hailsham apprehensively, the British constitution allows Parliament supreme power to alter the laws of the land at will. Or at least it did until recently. One of the most important recommendations of the Speaker's Commission is that a wide variety of people in authority, from judges to school teachers, should be required to understand the changes made to British law by the succession of treaties and international charters to which the UK became a signatory in recent years. It has been noticeable that a succession of individuals have, for example, turned to the European Court for redress against what they have seen as the oppressive operation of British justice. But law is one thing, democracy is another. It is theoretically possible to have a highly autocratic form of government with an equitable and effective system of law. Britain prides itself on its long history of democracy and believes that democracy is by far the best way to ensure that the law itself takes account of the changing aspirations and needs of the people. It is therefore essential that children at school learn about democracy and how to make it work. For politicians this apparently uncontroversial goal is fraught with problems.

How should we proceed? Schools themselves need to learn how to develop genuine responsibility for part of their operation to their pupils. Most have, of course, tried to do this ever since they began but their hands have been tied by a variety of constraints. Chief among these has been that they have had no effective control over their own resources. I argued above that it is positively harmful to appear to offer people a chance to affect the circumstances in which they live while in practice rendering it impossible for them to make any real change. Local Management of Schools provides the first real chance for schools to devolve to their pupils real resources and it is to be hoped that they will grasp the opportunity which this presents.

A second, and perhaps even more daunting constraint, is that of time. Every teacher knows that it is usually quicker to do something oneself than to wait until a committee has had a chance to deliberate on what needs to be done. This is pre-eminently true in schools, where each year brings in a new group to whom even the rudiments of democracy have to be introduced. At a time when school staffs are under huge pressure to devote more time to the National Curriculum and the assessments required under it, is it sensible even to consider asking schools to do more to familiarize their pupils with the workings of democracy? It is. Not only because every citizen ought to have some idea of how democracy affects his or her rights as a citizen but also because, if schools start with young enough children, the task of introducing effective democracy into the school will become progressively easier. One of the difficulties at present is that in many schools, one year is set aside for such excursions into non-curricular activity and this is both too short and often too late to be fully effective.

I am conscious that this policy requires a considerable leap of faith, not least by those politicians who love to excoriate schools for failing to teach 'the basics' and who will see in this proposal yet another distraction from the 'real' purpose of schools. They would be wrong to see it thus. Study after study, both in schools and in industry have shown that character traits such as self-confidence, the ability to work with others or to get others to work for one count for far more in the adult world than a store of information, much of which was out of date even as it was being imparted.

The next question is: can the system cope with a new generation which understands and is keen to use its understanding of democracy? In 1990 a multi-billion pound industry held an exhibition at Olympia. The UK Incentives industry is proud of itself. It has grown well beyond the point where it was to be seen as simply a rather tacky adjunct to the salesman's patter. It is now possible for the discerning customer to buy many products and services and attach to his purchase a 'gift' which is worth as much or more than the purchase itself. How can this be? The answer lies in the fact that less than 10 per cent of the customers can be bothered to fulfil the often simple conditions that are attached to the 'gift'. What they want is their purchase, and the knowledge that if they buy three or more of them over the next three months they can fly to the Everglades in Florida at the expense of the manufacturer does not interest them.

Democracy is much the same. It only works if most people take no interest in its workings. Take, for example, Britain's currently urgent need to find a balance between public consultation and planning imperatives if development is not to be paralysed. There are plenty of people prepared to suggest solutions to the problem which would exclude the public from having any serious say at all. Such people will pray in aid Pope's famous couplet:

> For forms of Government let fools contest;
> Whate'er is best administered is best.

And there is plenty of evidence to suggest that the public mostly supports Pope in his view.

Yet, to allow such a view to triumph is to acquiesce in precisely the kind of apathy which, as we have seen, opens the door to tyranny. However, fine sentiments are not enough. Every practising politician knows how difficult is has recently become to handle the huge increase in correspondence engendered by recent developments. These include: increased literacy in the population; better information through TV and other sources; a huge improvement in the sophistication at lobbying of many groups in society, especially the voluntary organizations whose membership is growing rapidly.

These are exactly the sort of changes which those of us who believe in teaching democracy as part of citizenship want to see, but there is no doubt that they call into question the whole present operation of our system of government. One has only to ask the question: do our constituents want us to spend so much time responding to individuals that we have no time to take part in national or international debate on the very issues which they have raised with us, to point the absurdity of carrying present trends too far. When I first entered politics Angus Maude told me how much he regretted what he called the 'Jack Ashley syndrome'. By this he meant that Clement Attlee's advice to new members: 'specialize (and keep out of the bars)' had led to a situation in which members felt that they could only be effective (as Jack Ashley has undoubtedly been effective) if they concentrate on narrow fields and take little or no part in the debates on the great constitutional issues of the day. Certainly those who have seen the emptiness of the House of Commons during debates on how much of our sovereignty should be passed to the European Community can bear witness to the aptness of Maude's regret.

The danger is that in seeking solutions to the problem of balancing the workload against the function to be performed we shall look for the wrong sorts of answer. Two anxieties, in particular, are worth recording. First, it may be thought that since backbenchers already carry a much smaller workload than ministers, efforts should be made further to insulate ministers from the day to day life of an MP. That is the route long ago chosen by the USA, for example, but it would certainly be a major change in Britain and its repercussions would include strengthening still further the Executive at the expense of the House as a whole. Second, it might be decided to provide MPs with more resources in their own offices and few MPs would turn such an offer down. Yet, to do so is merely to postpone working out the balance to be struck between the role of an MP and the public expectation of it. That is a debate we need to have and it would include the question of the size of constituencies in an age of much easier communications as well as the ways in which MPs can be empowered to represent more effectively their constituents to an Executive which is already more powerful than most MPs believe it should be.

No professional politician can write about democracy in Britain at the end of the twentieth century without commenting on the position of the political parties. It is a demonstrable and lamentable fact that only the irresponsibly radical parties attract any sizeable support from the young. As I have noted, this is to some extent balanced by the huge increases in membership among the young of many of the single-issue pressure groups. But single-issue groups rapidly become irresponsible in the sense that they feel few inhibitions in pressing their case regardless of the consequences for the wider society. Indeed, many young people feel strongly that politics, as conventionally practised, has become obsessed with forms which merely obstruct the implementation of policies which are so self-evidently good that almost any degree of single-minded devotion to them is appropriate, and if conventional politicians stand in the way they should be by-passed or forced to concede. That is the job of such lobbies and it is fair enough for them to press their case, but they make a lopsided tutor for their young members in the workings of democracy.

I believe that schools have an important role to play in explaining just how easy it is both to enter the main political parties in Britain and to climb the hierarchy within them. It is too easily forgotten that they are voluntary organizations in the purest sense of that phrase and, like voluntary organizations anywhere, are desperate for new members. When I worked at Conservative Central Office I watched one young man rise to be Chairman of the national Young Conservatives with a seat on all the central committees of the National Party in three short years. There is no point in waiting for the parties to change to become more glamorous to young people. They never will because they are dominated by people who have neither the skills nor the desire to change in that way. All that is required is for the young themselves to enter the party of their choice and take over those parts of it which seem to them desirable. In doing so they will discover how important it is to fit their own preoccupation into the wider political context.

Finally, what chance is there of any of this working out in practice? Are all these suggestions destined to fall on stony ground like so many exhortations to hard-pressed schools in the past? I believe that there are real grounds for believing that progress can be made. Chief among them is the evidence submitted to the Commission by the editor of this book that the young themselves are anxious to know more about their status as citizens. It would make a change to run the education system in response to requests from the young, but as we move slowly down the road to local accountability the wishes of the young may start to figure in the design of the school day. Second, there is the growing evidence that success in adult life depends more on the display of qualities likely to be fostered by education about the rights and duties of citizens, and the programmes needed to give practical support to that teaching. At every level of British life there is a growing need for self-confident individuals who understand that their fulfilment depends as much on what they do with and for others as on what they do solely for themselves.

There is one other crucially important consideration. All our hopes and expectations for our future as British citizens depend on the assumption that our economy will go on growing. That is why, however hesitantly, we have agreed to join the European Community

124

and that is why we move so slowly to relieve the pressure points in British society, such as racial disputes. We assume that economic growth will massage them away as it has mostly done in the past. I believe that that is a dangerous assumption to rely on. Sooner or later, in a world increasingly threatened by population growth and increasingly aware of how finite are its resources, our style of democracy will have to adapt to a falling standard of living and there are precious few signs that any of our politicians would know how to run such a campaign. If our young are prevented by our lack of imagination and trust from learning how to make democracy work, their status as citizens may well be snatched away from them by the emotions generated among an unprepared population as living standards fall year after year.

The time to address such matters is surely now.

References

Fogelman, K. (1990) 'Citizenship in secondary schools: a national survey', Appendix E, in Commission on Citizenship, *Encouraging Citizenship*. London: HMSO.

Halpern, D. (1990) 'Active citizenship and a healthy society'. Paper prepared for the Commission on Citizenship.